Jane Austen
and
the State

✻✻✻

Jane Austen
and
the State

✻✻✻

MARY EVANS

Tavistock Publications
London and New York

First published in 1987 by
Tavistock Publications Ltd
11 New Fetter Lane, London EC4P 4EE

Published in the USA by
Tavistock Publications
in association with Methuen, Inc.
29 West 35th Street, New York NY 10001

Printed in Great Britain by Richard Clay Ltd. Bungay, Suffolk

British Library Cataloguing in Publication Data
Evans, Mary, 1946–
Jane Austen and the state
1. Austen, Jane — Criticism and interpretation
I. Title
823'.7   PR4037

ISBN 0-422-61370—3

Library of Congress Cataloguing in Publication Data
Evans, Mary, 1946–
Jane Austen and the state.

Bibliography: p.
Includes indexes.
1. Austen, Jane, 1775–1817—Political and social views.
2. Social problems in literature.
3. Politics in literature.
4. Capitalism and literature.
5. Economics in literature.
I. Title.
PR4038.P6E9   1987   823'.7   86–30196

ISBN 0-422-61370-3

*To David, Thomas, and
James Alexander*

Contents

Acknowledgements

This essay was written partly in the United States whilst I was a guest of Martha and James Davis at John Winthrop House, Harvard University. I would like to thank both Martha and Jim for their hospitality and many kindnesses. Mrs Sue Macdonald typed the manuscript with great good humour and accuracy and Gill Davies provided valuable editorial support and assistance. I discussed many of the ideas in the essay with David Morgan and I would like to thank him for his enthusiastic and perceptive contributions to these discussions.

Introduction

In Jane Austen's last novel, *Persuasion*, the heroine remarks
that literature is a poor guide to human behaviour and that
books cannot prove anything. The conversation in which the
remark occurs concerns the question of the greater or lesser
capacity for emotional commitment of men and women; one
of the characters attempts to demonstrate his case by
reference to literature and is immediately told, by a strong
authorial voice, that literature is no guide to life. What was
true for England in the early nineteenth century is just as
true today: Jane Austen's novels are not themselves factual
accounts of life as it was lived but brilliant discussions of the
issue of personal behaviour within the context of capitalist
social relations.

That issue remains consistently pertinent in England in
the 1980s, at a point in our history where it would appear that
the increased impoverishment of a large section of the population, particularly the female population, is due in large part
to the deliberate policies of a democratically elected government. Jane Austen would probably find it difficult to fault the
formal procedure which brought to power a government
officially committed to monetarism and the curtailment of
the state's responsibilities for welfare provision; but she
might have questioned the policies themselves, and their
underlying assumptions.

This is not to suggest that Jane Austen belongs in any
sense to a tradition of the 'Left' – or indeed any other formal
contemporary political grouping – but it does mean that the

values she endorses are incompatible with the practices and policies of contemporary Toryism, particularly because of her concern for the protection of women and children, and for the articulation of their rights and views. (As she remarks in *Persuasion*, 'Men have had every advantage of us in telling their own story. Education has been theirs in so much higher a degree; the pen has been in their hands.'[1]) Unlike some Victorian novelists Jane Austen does not argue that women are helpless victims; on the contrary she maintains that they are active makers of their fate. But what she does show is the vulnerability of women in the economic market-place, a vulnerability that leads to the paradox of both their in-adequate protection (in the sense of real provision for their needs and those of their children) and their excessive restriction (in terms of their inferior civil liberties and assumptions about female dependence).

In demonstrating, in each of her novels, the potential harshness of the market economy, Jane Austen establishes herself as a major figure in European realism. We can read her novels as novels of manners, as light entertainment about a vanished world, but to do so is to ignore the central concern of the author not for manners, but for morality and for the establishment of a morality that can survive in a world which is increasingly hostile to all interests other than the purely economic. As Jane Austen recognized, the bourgeois world is particularly skilful at presenting economic self-interest as morality ('freedom', for example, can often be translated as the right to unregulated entrepreneurial activity) and one of the reiterated themes of her novels is the misnaming by some of her characters of actions that they know to be guided by simple self-interest. Her morality, therefore, is not consoling but is one of absolute principle and absolute honesty: a morality which demands that characters should behave in ways which they would often rather avoid or dismiss.

But against what may appear as harsh and unbending judgements we have to allow that Jane Austen's ideal world is one in which individuals would be assured of the mutual

Introduction

fulfilment of obligations and responsibilities, a world in which poverty would be recognized and alleviated, and injustice righted. The scale of these mutual obligations in Jane Austen's fictional world is, in an empirical sense, fairly small (rather more than the four or five families that she outlined as the basis for her fiction but rather less than entirely inclusive of English society as a whole),[2] but the implications of her ideas about proper moral behaviour are general. Unlike later novelists Jane Austen does not set out blueprints for society which translate the individual into the passive instrument of social ideals; on the contrary she argues that individuals, and communities of individuals, make society what it is. People, Jane Austen might have remarked, make their own history. As she might also have said, they do so against both a personal and a social history, but it is a complete abdication of all personal and moral responsibility to argue that people cannot make choices, or that they are entirely made by circumstances. To adopt this position, as Jane Austen recognized, is merely to adopt the dominant values of the age: values – in the eighteenth as much as in the twentieth century – of materialism and individual self-interest. The seductive power of these values, for individuals and governments, was acknowledged by Jane Austen as considerable. But what she also acknowledged was the human capacity for commitment to others, for the disinterested care and comfort of the vulnerable, and for resistance to those social pressures which elevated the process of material accumulation to the ideological status of absolute human and moral reality.

1
The world of
Jane Austen

The association of Jane Austen and the state at first appears
an unlikely one. Of all English novelists, Austen is generally
assumed to be the most resistant to attempts by feminists,
marxists, and sociologically minded literary critics to establish relationships between a literary work and a particular
social formation. Whilst Austen's near contemporaries, such
as the Brontës and George Eliot, can be plundered success-
fully for information about the 1832 Reform Act, industrial
unrest in the early days of the British factory system, or the
conditions of work of Victorian governesses, Austen remains
aloof from attempts to cull from her pages specific facts about
social life and existent or emergent ideologies. As numerous
critics have pointed out, we can search in vain in Austen for
discussion of the great contextual events of her lifetime: the
French Revolution and the Napoleonic Wars are virtually
absent. What we find instead are those neat ladies and
gentlemen (as Charlotte Brontë described them) who per-
ambulate endlessly on well-cut lawns, involved in endless
conversational games designed to ensure that the more
eligible single people marry each other. Indeed, in some
circles an admiration for Jane Austen's work could be
interpreted as identification with the views of Lord David
Cecil and other Tory Janeites: a nostalgia for a golden age of
the English gentry when elegant manners dictated and
organized a coherent and ordered social world. To such
enthusiasts Mrs Norris is merely 'comic' and the rescue from
penury by marriage of Fanny Price and Jane Fairfax accords

with romantic notions that deserving women should be recognized, courted, and married by good and honourable men.

The purpose of this essay is not, however, to challenge this extreme Janeite view of Jane Austen. As the author herself might have said, such a view scarcely requires rational opposition, and recent critics (for example Marilyn Butler (1975), Alistair Duckworth (1971), and Margaret Kirkham (1983)) have done much to demonstrate that Jane Austen was deeply involved in, and cognizant of, the major ideological debates of her time. But the crucial debate, I shall argue, with which she was concerned was the issue of morality, and in particular the question of how individuals should assess their personal responsibilities and inclinations in the light of their material circumstances. Thus the central thesis of this essay is that Jane Austen offers her readers a radical morality, and that far from endorsing the given, and emergent, values of late eighteenth-century capitalism she was in many ways deeply critical of them. The taken-for-granted association of Austen with conservatism – a position echoed even by those critics who have located Austen in a social context – misinterprets, I wish to suggest, two central themes of Austen's fiction: her attempt to elucidate a morality that is independent of the material values of the capitalist marketplace, and the claims that she articulates for the equality of men and women and the right of women to moral independence and autonomy. In the context of developments in the British state's organization and regulation of morality in the late eighteenth and early nineteenth centuries Austen represents not a conservative but a liberal tradition: a tradition opposed to the equation of moral worth with wealth, and to the extension of patriarchal authority.

Morality is, of course, a crucial problem for any social system: how does a particular society ensure that its members behave in ways that are appropriate to its specific form of social life? Moreover, how are disputes between individuals, involving conflicts between their interests, decided in ways that guarantee social order, coherence, and continuity? All these problems are well known to anthropologists and sociologists, and are identified as central areas of concern. The resolution of disputes, and the elaboration of moral codes and rules of interpersonal behaviour, are part and parcel of the appropriate subject matter of social scientists; from this perspective, therefore, the novels of Jane Austen immediately become a rich and vital source of information about a particular social group. The 'tribe' – if we can call them that – of later eighteenth and early nineteenth-century gentry can be a source of endless fascination: encapsulated for ever in the pages of fiction they can be analysed with a thoroughness that is difficult to replicate in the case of real human subjects. But this attitude to Austen's characters overlooks one crucial factor: this group of people are not inventions, neither did they live in a historical or social no person's land. On the contrary, Austen's characters lived at a crucial point in English history: the point at which a society which was already essentially capitalist was undergoing transformation into an industrial society – a society in which the accumulation of profit was to assume a new, and more comprehensive, ruthlessness. It was not, of course, that the agricultural magnates or merchants of the eighteenth century were against capital accumulation or uninterested in the rewards of wealth. This was demonstrably not the case. But the transformation of England into an industrial capitalist society involved the thorough integration of all aspects of social and material life into a form of order compatible with the demands of a society geared to the maximization of profit. As other social scientists have already pointed out, the period between 1780 and 1840 was a crucial locus in English history in terms of the increasing sophistication and comprehensiveness of attempts by the state to order and regulate the lives of its citizens. A largely rural world of agricultural production gave way – albeit slowly and only generally by the end of the nineteenth century – to an urban world of mechanized industrial production, a world in which people lived in concentrations of population and had to be controlled and organized in ways other than by the traditional community restraints of the countryside.

But Austen's social world, it must be emphasized, is not one in which the coming of industrialization threatens rural calm and stability. First, rural calm and stability are ideological constructs of romantic historians: the history of the European countryside is crowded with conflicts between landowners and peasants, between different class groups, and between diverse cultures. Second, it was not industrialization which immediately threatened Austen's social world but the increasing commercialization of agriculture and the resources of the land in the eighteenth century. In a major and important essay on the social location of Austen's world Terry Lovell (1978) has pointed out that Austen herself belonged to the lesser gentry, a social group whose prosperity was increasingly threatened as the rise of capitalism in the countryside proceeded along its unimpeded path. As Lovell writes:

'Different sections of the gentry class were able to adapt to their new social role with varying degrees of ease or hardship. Squeezed between the rising capitalist tenant-farmer and the upper gentry, whose estates had been consolidated and increased in size at their expense, the lesser gentry, to which Jane Austen's family belonged, was in a more exposed position. A position from which the perception of a general threat to their class might be perceived, from which the social and ideological differences between traditional rural society and the new urban capitalist order would appear very great.'

(Lovell 1978: 21)

Austen, Lovell argues, is thus not writing from a position of security. On the contrary, she is writing from a position of insecurity, in which her own situation could easily become that of Miss Bates in *Emma* and in which it was easy to

understand the restrictions imposed by a limited and unreliable income. The Janeite view of Jane Austen overlooks,
perhaps not entirely surprisingly, the material problems of
many of Austen's characters, and indeed of Austen herself.
Equally, those critics who have attempted to rescue Austen
from her over-genteel enthusiasts have in their own way
given a false emphasis to her novels – that of supposing that
Austen is first and foremost an ideological writer, in the
sense of being exclusively concerned with questions of
individual morality or personal behaviour. D.W. Harding, in
his famous essay 'Regulated Hatred: an Aspect of the Work of
Jane Austen' (1963), offers an almost Laingian analysis of
Austen's portrayal of family relationships – an analysis
which is acute and perceptive in its revelation of the
intensity of feeling in Austen, but which nevertheless fails to
locate a major source of those deeply felt passions, namely,
the desire to maintain and, if possible, improve an increasingly precarious position in the social world. To call this
materialism might suggest an interpretation which is solely
and simply about income: on the contrary, I would argue that
Austen's materialism is far more sophisticated than this. Of
course she can see as clearly as any intelligent observer of
the social world that income is necessary to maintain life,
and a certain level of income is essential to maintain a way of
life that allows for the employment of servants and reasonably acceptable accommodation. But more than this, she
realizes that income maintains not just the material world
but also the social world: without that sufficient income there
is no access to social networks, to assembly, to literature, to
even limited mobility. The very fabric of daily life, of food, of
dress, of light and heat, is thus implied and considered by
Jane Austen: she can not only locate as clearly as any
capitalist the extent of an individual's income, but can also
see beyond the bare facts of cash in the hand to what income,
or its lack, can make of life. When Mr Knightley, in *Emma*,
challenges Emma's treatment of Miss Bates, Jane Austen
makes him remark that she 'is poor; she has sunk from the

comforts she was born to; and, if she live to old age, must probably sink more!'[1] Lack of income here is given a reality and a human perception that could not be described simply in terms of lack of money. 'She has sunk from the comforts she was born to' suggests precisely the decline in fortune of Miss Bates: the loss, in adulthood and early old age, of any expectation of easy sufficiency and the constant threat not merely of financial stringency but of actual material hardship.

So far from a position of security, and an experience of little except ease and prosperity, the actual experience of Jane Austen, and many of her characters, is that of possible material hardship and constraint. The mythologizers of her world have perceived only Mr Darcy, Mr Knightley, and Emma Woodhouse: the other, more numerous, characters – the Dashwoods, the Bennets, Fanny Price and the entire Price family, the family of Sir Walter Elliot, and Miss Bates and her mother – are all people who live if not actually in poverty, in the sense that it was experienced by sections of the eighteenth-century peasantry or urban poor, then at least uncomfortably close to the possibility of becoming poor and consequently far removed from bourgeois society. There are admittedly very real differences in the degree of possible hardship to be faced by Miss Bates and Sir Walter Elliot: Miss Bates could end her life in abject poverty in one room, whilst Sir Walter faces exile from his ancestral home, but still a reasonably prosperous future in furnished rooms. But the essential similarity uniting these characters is that both live a life that is far from absolutely secure; there has to be, for each character in her or his different way, a daily calculation of the means of maintaining ordinary life. Sir Walter, as Jane Austen points out more than once, has brought insecurity and the threat of insolvency upon himself through his extravagance and profligacy, and is almost too arrogant to realize that he might become poor. Nevertheless, his relationships with others become coloured by the decline in his fortunes: Captain Wentworth, once an unacceptable son-in-law, becomes at least tolerable when the possessor of a large capital sum.

An examination of many of the other characters of Jane Austen's novels would demonstrate the same possible insecurities as those faced by Sir Walter Elliot or Miss Bates. Thus her novels might be read as a form of suspense drama: what would happen to Anne Elliot, to Elizabeth and Jane Bennet, to Fanny Price, and the Dashwood sisters if suitable, and in most cases either wealthy or comfortably off, husbands had not appeared on the scene? Anne Elliot had nothing, her livelihood depended on an idle and spendthrift father; equally, the Bennet and the Dashwood sisters had little or no provision for their maintenance. Mrs Bennet in *Pride and Prejudice* is generally regarded as one of the more absurd and comic figures of English fiction, and her preoccupation with marrying off her daughters as the mania of a somewhat inadequate intelligence. But in view of the economic exigencies facing the unmarried daughters of the eighteenth-century gentry, Mrs Bennet's concerns do not seem entirely ridiculous. Indeed, her obsessive concern with marriage and her ceaseless – and quite ruthless – pursuit of young men to marry her daughters are arguably instances of greater parental responsibility than the sardonic lack of interest of Mr Bennet, to whom the activities of his wife are nothing but an irritation. If Mrs Bennet is slightly crazy, then perhaps she is so because she perceives, more clearly than her husband, the possible fate of her daughters if they do not marry. Mr Bennet, by far the more attractive character on a first (or even a second) reading of the novel, could then be interpreted as an irresponsible patriarch: a man with so little real interest in the fate of his daughters that he is content to allow his wife to bear the brunt of anxiety about their future. Given that she has five daughters, it is little wonder that at times Mrs Bennet is less than rational.

So the apparent ease and comfort of Jane Austen's world can be rapidly revealed as one of limited and unreliable security. Capitalism, as much in the eighteenth as in the twentieth century, is not a stable social system: its perpetual crises and problematic continuation condemn those who live within it to endless concern about the maintenance of material life. As if to emphasize this point, Jane Austen herself provides, in all the novels, minor characters, who often play little part in the central narrative and yet stand as embodiments of the fate of women handicapped by poverty or social stigma. Outside the cultivated and elegant gardens, the splendid drawing rooms, therefore, are the shades of real hardship. Thus in *Mansfield Park* we find the Price family living in squalor in Portsmouth, in *Persuasion* Anne Elliot's friend Mrs Smith living in cramped poverty, Colonel Brandon's ruined sister-in-law Eliza eking out her days in what is described as a 'spunging' house, and of course Miss Bates and her mother in *Emma* confined to their small flat and dependent on Mr Knightley and Emma for minimal comforts. If women do not marry and do not live by the moral code of bourgeois society then their fate is unlikely to be prosperous or happy.

Whether or not this account of the lives of women in the late eighteenth century replicates actual social reality is a point which it would be difficult to establish with absolute certainty. But what we can deduce from historical record is that with very few exceptions (Emma Woodhouse being one) women in eighteenth-century England – be they members of the gentry, the urban middle class, or the rural poor – needed to marry in order to guarantee for themselves economic support. Women who belonged to the gentry or the aristocracy were certainly provided with capital sums (and Austen documents very clearly the capital sums owned by her heroines) but with one exception these were small sums and largely insufficient to maintain a household. So women could, and did, have incomes, but for accommodation and the expenses of running their household they were largely dependent on men: initially their fathers and subsequently, it was to be hoped, their husbands. Paid employment did not exist for middle-class women: in *Emma* Jane Fairfax nearly becomes a governess, but that is the only professional option mentioned by Austen. We can now show that it was far from being the single profession open to eighteenth-century women; but the forms of paid employment available to middle-class women were nevertheless limited and the question voiced to women in many households, in all classes and to this day, of 'who do you think is going to keep you?' was clearly a dominating concern of women of Jane Austen's class and social milieu.

That the question of potential responsibility for material provision for women is still voiced today is a demonstration of the consistency and resilience of a pattern of relationships between the sexes over a period of some hundred years. The pattern is that of female dependence on male provision – the expectation that men will provide the material conditions of life for women. This expectation has persisted despite the development of an industrial society, universal education, the accessibility of contraception, the extension of civil liberties to women, and the other numerous changes that have altered the lives of men and women in the last 200 years. Yet what has not changed is the different access that the sexes have to public power and public life: a contemporary Captain Wentworth might still make his fortune with greater ease than a contemporary Anne Elliot, and it is still left to men to manage the affairs of women. Nevertheless, it is as much the case today as it was in the time of Jane Austen that women exercise power over matters that affect individuals, and individual households. Moreover, they do this, in the 1980s as much as in the late eighteenth century, in the general context of capitalist social relations. And the social relationships of capital unite the sexes as much then as now; whatever the marital conflicts of Mr and Mrs John Dashwood in *Sense and Sensibility* it is apparent that interest in their property will forge a link impervious to any divisions of gender. Indeed, far from acting as a sister to her husband's sister-in-law, Mrs John Dashwood behaves towards her with the cold-blooded ruthlessness of a determined and callous entrepreneur. The needs of capital, in this instance, take precedence over any consideration of personal concern or moral responsibility.

We have then in Austen's work a picture of a world in which the majority of characters are constrained, to a greater or lesser extent, by material necessity, and in which the assessment of material need is acted out against the background of a society in which material ruin is a possibility. Within this context it is generally the case, then as now, that women have less power than men over their immediate material conditions and general political circumstances. Women did not, in the late eighteenth century, any more than they do today, exercise political or material power that was equal or equivalent to that of men. The question of how women are to act, how they are to maintain their interests, consequently becomes crucial to any author with more than a passing interest in relationships between the sexes. Indeed, an examination of the eighteenth-century novel suggests that just as much as Austen – and later, Eliot and the Brontës – male authors were much exercised with the question of the development of a viable morality of sexual relationships. Terry Eagleton (1982) has, for example, persuasively argued that Richardson's *Clarissa* is an extended discussion of the possibilities of female resistance to the demands of an assertive, aggressive patriarchal culture that is increasingly regarded as entirely legitimate. Clarissa's resistance to Lovelace, her demonstration that the values of Lovelace and her own relatives are highly questionable, indicate a deep suspicion of both bourgeois self-interest and aristocratic sexual codes. Eagleton writes:

> 'Clarissa superbly "totalizes" the sexual and the social, conscious of what we might today call the "relative autonomy" of sexual oppression while materialist enough to discern its economic basis. Sexuality, far from being some displacement of class conflict, is the very medium in which it is conducted.'
>
> (Eagleton 1982: 88)

10

The world of Jane Austen

The complexities of the relationships between the characters in *Clarissa* are such that it is impossible to distinguish characters who act simply in terms of their class or their gender interests. Certainly what Richardson is able to show is that no one solution exists to the dilemmas that confront Clarissa and Lovelace. If Clarissa agrees to Lovelace's demands, she then compromises her sense of self and her autonomy: patriarchy, or the code of sexual relationships as construed by Lovelace, offers women no opportunity for the development of their own perception of sexuality and its place in human relationships. If, on the other hand, she rejects Lovelace in the terms of the bourgeois morality of the Harlowes, then she does so in terms that are, to her, deeply morally suspect in that they make social convenience and self-interest into morality. The Harlowes' morality, or their moral advice to women, is that of the market – the guide to behaviour that suggests that women should never enter heterosexual relationships unless some bargain has been struck that offers material protection. This form of moral advice contains, of course, an element of real protection for women and as such is a code that is not without its positive side even outside the context of bourgeois self-interest, for it offers women the understanding that the children who may result from sexual relationships will be recognized by their fathers and entitled to their protection and support. But this ancient and generally agreed morality, which provided a pattern for the organization of sexual relations throughout Europe for centuries, is only part of the code of the late eighteenth-century bourgeoisie – and it is fundamentally different in one respect, for what is at stake is less the protection of women and children than of property and status.

So we cannot identify the bourgeois morality of the Harlowes as positive, or say that it is superior to that of Lovelace. The codes are different but neither is acceptable to those concerned (as Clarissa is) with an ethically viable morality. And all that Richardson can offer as a way out of the moral, and indeed personal, impasse in which Clarissa finds herself, is death – a slow, masochistic death in which her hatred of the many forces that oppose her is turned into a self-destroying depression that eventually saps her vitality and her will to live. Quite what else Clarissa could have done in her situation is an interesting question for speculation: in other novels in which heroines have been faced with equally appalling choices they have taken equally radical actions (a flight, like Jane Eyre's, in Charlotte Brontë's novel, more or less literally across the heather or a deliberate flouting of convention by satirizing – as did Catherine Earnshaw in *Wuthering Heights* – the expectations of Victorian society about romance and marriage) or else have failed – like Tolstoy's Anna Karenina – to transcend the limits of their situation and live outside bourgeois convention. Anna's suicide, like Clarissa's death, is both an act of a tortured individual and an act against the society which has created the miseries that the individual has endured. Clarissa's death destroys Lovelace as much as Anna's destroys Vronsky: these dramatic situations, in which strong passions and strong wills are irreconcilably opposed, represent the conflicts that result in societies, and more particularly in classes within societies, where moral codes are contradictory and inconsistent.

But the morality of sexuality occupies a crucial place in the concerns of a society which values social order and coherence. It is unlikely that the specific dilemma of Clarissa was widely replicated in late eighteenth-century England, but nevertheless Richardson's dramatization of the conflict between Lovelace and Clarissa does represent an extremely important conflict between two groups within the English ruling class. To quote Eagleton again:

'the tragedy of Clarissa . . . dramatises a collision between two wings of the eighteenth century ruling class whose true destiny lay not in conflict but in alliance. In ideological terms, however, the tragedy is indeed of "world-

The world of Jane Austen

historical" proportions, a key phase of English class
history. Lovelace is a reactionary throwback, an old-style
libertine or Restoration relic who resists a proper "em-
bourgeoisement"; the future of the English aristocracy lies
not with him but with the impeccably middle-class Sir
Charles Grandison.'

(Eagleton 1982: 89)

Not of course, that by the beginning of the nineteenth
century every aristocrat had been transformed into a model of
bourgeois propriety, or even that every aristocrat had
behaved like Lovelace in the eighteenth century. What is at
stake here is not the literal correspondence of fictional
behaviour with the behaviour of real people, but the credence
and viability given to different moralities at different times.
The question of 'how to live' is therefore not one that is
'solved' by either Richardson or Austen, but is an enduring
question which is given different answers as circumstances
and situations change.

Between Richardson and Austen there lies, however, the
very significant difference that whilst Richardson's major
heroine dies a death of slow misery, Austen leaves her
heroines at the end of her novels in positions of unassailable
virtue – and generally much enhanced social and material
circumstances. Since Austen is as aware as Richardson that
there are problems to be raised and questions asked about the
appropriate nature of sexual morality, we might conclude
that she develops some better answers to the question. Yet
such a reading would ignore the differences between Austen
and Richardson in their conceptualization of the problems
involved: Richardson presents us with dichotomous groups
and polarizes the two central characters in *Clarissa* in terms
of their values and interests. Men and women – represented
by Lovelace and Clarissa – thus stand as two separate groups
and between them there is, Richardson suggests, a conflict
that is as old as human history. Austen, on the other hand,
juxtaposes not men and women, but types of human beings: to

use the titles of her own novels, the proud and the prejudiced, the sensible and the oversensible. Gender therefore becomes secondary to the nature of a human being's personal qualities: the battle is less for control of sexual access than for the terms in which sexual access is agreed.

This battle was – and is – a crucial one for both men and women and for social order. As suggested above, a moral code has existed within western European peasant communities for centuries about the proper conduct of sexual relationships: pre-marital heterosexual relationships were not barred (although frequently not condoned either) but the community did expect men to acknowledge and support the children resulting from such relationships. Pre-marital chastity, for both men and women, was therefore less of an issue for agricultural workers or landless labourers than it was for the middle class, the gentry, and the aristocracy. At stake of course are different priorities; for the poor the major concern is that children be provided for, and that women will be assured of material support. For the propertied classes, the major concern is that property should be passed from one generation to the next: ensuring legitimate heirs, and the clear identity of the father, are thus of importance. In these classes, therefore, sexual relationships have to be carefully organized so that rights to property are clearly defined.

Yet sexual relationships and marriage are not, for any class or group in any historical period, solely about material concerns. Also involved are the individual's expectations about sexual and emotional life and the nature of the obligations that individuals enter into when they marry. The Church of England – in much the same way as the Roman Catholic Church – makes no secret of its views when it places 'mutual help and support' of husband and wife in third place on the list of duties involved in marriage. The text of the Anglican marriage service, written at a time when the association of heterosexual intercourse with reproduction was difficult to escape, made it quite clear that the protection (and the birth) of children was the church's major priority. If we read 'children' as a metaphor for fertility, or for procreation, we then see that the church is advocating, indeed supporting, the control and regulation of human fertility in a particular way which has become the accepted pattern of British society. This involves the legal marriage of a man and a woman and the absolute, and as yet unbroken, responsibility of the husband to support his wife and children. Nor do responsibilities solely fall on husbands: the wife, the marriage service makes clear, is expected to 'obey' her husband; authority within marriage is clearly located in men.

From historical record and biography, it is possible to deduce that the expectations of the church about people's behaviour within marriage were disappointed as often in the eighteenth century as they are in the twentieth: husbands and wives did not honour, love, or support one another, nor did they necessarily forsake all others. So the reality of behaviour in these areas was often far from the ideal. Equally, it was frequently the case that husbands did not support their families: women and children were deserted and left penniless, and surviving accounts of family and domestic life suggest that the 'problems' of the family are no invention of the latter part of the twentieth century. All such possibilities were inevitably known to Jane Austen, whose family and friendship network was both extensive and varied. Indeed, she saw in her lifetime an outstanding example of the complete rejection of conventional expectations of morality in the Prince Regent's behaviour to his wife. Not only did the Prince Regent flout bourgeois conventions about monogamous marriage, he also flouted aristocratic convention in the open and deliberate presentation of his mistress in the place of his wife. As Edward VIII was to discover some hundred years later, London aristocratic society could tolerate adultery and extramarital relationships of considerable length and commitment, but it could not tolerate notoriety, publicity, lack of discretion, or attempts by individuals to translate relationships established outside marriage into relationships that would be those of marriage.

What these two particular instances suggest is that the

organization of sexuality and sexual relations is both a problem for bourgeois society in the literal sense – that of any society's need to maintain the organization of fertility and reproduction – and in the more complex sense of the need of bourgeois society to organize the moral categories of its citizens. This concern pays little attention to the quality of the order that is maintained: what is at stake is the maintenance of viable categories of 'good' and 'bad'. Thus, for example, in the case of the relationships of the Prince Regent and Edward VIII with women to whom they were not married, the issue was not only one of social order, but also of the kind of behaviour that an individual could legitimately adopt in order to ensure his or her happiness. In both cases, numerous individuals and institutions were much exercised at the behavour of the individuals involved; in both cases the individuals apparently endorsed the belief that people have a right to the pursuit of happiness.

The naïvety, in both the social and the moral sense, of this belief is one of the chief targets of Austen's fiction. She demonstrates, in all her novels, that individuals are very often poor judges of what will make them happy, and that the individual pursuit of happiness and of perceived needs will frequently bring unhappiness on innocent others. But her moral sense is not one of prohibition. Unlike some later Victorian (and Edwardian and twentieth-century) moralists Austen does not stand in the tradition of either condemnation and prohibition or of bourgeois moral rigidity. She is not, therefore, a friend to the morality of the Harlowes, nor, we can assume, a supporter of the kind of bourgeois morality which, in Victorian Britain, was responsible for the Contagious Diseases Act and the stigmatization of illegitimate children and their mothers. From a background of relative security and social assurance, Austen suggests to us that morality is not to be enforced; it has to be taught, and learned. Moreover, a moral act and a moral decision cannot be motivated by inclination, or by what are described in the twentieth century as 'feelings'. 'Feelings', as Jane Austen was well aware, are far from adequate as a guide to human action. The morality of Austen's work is one that is, I hope to show, not only radical in its assumptions about the moral equality of the sexes, but also, and perhaps more importantly, radical in so far as she suggests that the social relationships of bourgeois society are empty and meaningless if they are devoid of moral principle and concern. That Austen does not question capitalism or heterosexuality must be acknowledged – what she does is to make for both patterns of social organization moral systems that have an internal coherence and ethical viability. To say that she defends capitalism and heterosexuality is thus far from accurate; capitalism and heterosexuality as we know them are social systems that have been fashioned in ways which Austen would have regarded as unacceptable. For example, although Austen is not a critic of material gain, she is a fierce critic of material greed and ruthlessness. The unacceptable face of capitalism appears more than once in her novels: she is clearly against the exploitative entrepreneur, and suggests that the pursuit of profit must be tempered by moral concern and values other than those of the profit motive. So we are faced with an intriguing problem: is Austen suggesting that a morality of personal relationships can be developed, within the context of capitalist social relationships, that is independent of the material relationships of that society? If so, does it then follow that what she develops is a morality appropriate for all classes, and both sexes, within capitalism? The following pages explore these issues.

2

Property relations

One of the taboos of polite English bourgeois society is about the discussion of money: well-bred people do not talk about the source of their income. According to this rule, Jane Austen is neither genteel nor well-bred, for all her novels demonstrate a most unladylike concern with the income of her characters. Thus whilst Charlotte Brontë is content to describe Mr Rochester as 'wealthy' in *Jane Eyre*, Jane Austen has no such inhibitions about situating Mr Darcy *et al.* very clearly and precisely in the material world. In the first seven chapters of *Pride and Prejudice* Jane Austen tells us exactly how much money Mr Darcy, Mr Bingley, and Mr Bennet possess: moreover, we know their different sources of income and are thus able to locate them within different sections of the English bourgeoisie. In the same novel we also find that although Jane Austen allows one of her sterling male characters to be a traditional landowner, she does not associate virtue solely with the possession of land or with an income drawn from agriculture. Hence she is no anti-trade conservative; on the contrary, trade and professional activity are positively endorsed.

Her attitude to money, therefore, is not one of straightforward endorsement of established wealth: a concern of her fiction is to demonstrate and articulate a morality which endorses the responsibility of male individuals to maintain themselves and their dependents and yet demands that no character – male or female – should be motivated in their actions solely by material concerns. To be materially irresponsible is, to Jane Austen, a sign of moral failing, just as an over-interest in money suggests greed and a false set of priorities. In all, she demonstrates a belief in maintaining property, and in securing a harmonious relationship between material and moral prosperity. It is a view of life which values care and consensus in human relationships: resolve questions about material existence by greed or carelessness, she argues, and the potential harmony of social life is distorted. To maintain oneself is a human responsibility: for men the responsibility takes the form of the obligation to provide a sufficient income for a household, for women the duty is to organize the proper expenditure of the income. It is not an ethic which endorses the enjoyment of wealth without the earning of wealth, equally it is not an ethic which excuses material calculation through subjective perceived need.

That money, and material existence, are both central issues in Austen's fiction needs emphasis, since her work has often been read as distant from the real concerns of the material world.[1] Yet in every novel characters appear who direct their lives – and often those of others – by naked material self-interest. There can be few other passages in fiction which so forcefully record the power of human greed over human responsibility as the passage in *Sense and Sensibility* in which Mrs John Dashwood justifies the miserly provision of help for Mrs Dashwood and her daughters. Inclined to provide assistance, Mr Dashwood is swayed by the arguments of his wife:

'Indeed, to say the truth, I am convinced within myself that your father had no idea of your giving them any money at all. The assistance he thought of, I dare say, was only such as might be reasonably expected of you; for instance such as looking out for a comfortable small house for them, helping them to move their things, and sending them presents of fish and game, and so forth, whenever they are in season. I'll lay my life that he meant nothing further; indeed, it would be very strange and unreasonable if he did!'[2]

19

Jane Austen and the State

This mixture of powerful greed, apparent sincerity ('I'll lay my life'), and reference to a general law of behaviour ('it would be very strange and unreasonable if he did') wins the day, and John Dashwood's vague inclinations towards generosity disappear. A central theme of *Sense and Sensibility* is, therefore, material greed and its effect on individual behaviour: Mrs John Dashwood, Lucy Steele, and Willoughby are all primarily motivated by financial gain.

So in her first published novel, Jane Austen suggests to us a concern which is to recur throughout the rest of her work: how to balance moral and material concerns. A survey of her work reveals that she has a diverse experience of the means by which members of the late eighteenth-century gentry, bourgeoisie, and aristocracy maintain themselves and that her social range is far greater than an impressionistic study of her works might suggest. It is true that Jane Austen includes at least one large country estate in all her novels, but around the country seat are clustered men who maintain themselves through the church (always the Church of England), the army and the navy, trade, and the professions. Some of these men – for example Colonel Brandon in *Sense and Sensibility* – derive income from country estates (and in his case actually possess one) although they are not defined solely in terms of their relationship to the land. But whilst there is a range of possible activity for men in Austen, no such range exists for women: women, in the novels, are attached to landed estates through men, and only the possibility of employment as a governess (for Jane Fairfax in *Emma*) is suggested as an alternative activity for women to that of daughter, wife, and mother. If women possess property, it is capital: Emma is the wealthiest of Austen's female characters, and something of an exception, for it is generally the case that the women characters possess, in their own right, less than the men. Such a situation reflects, accurately enough, the social reality of the period: estates were, in general, entailed on a male (usually the eldest) child, whilst daughters were provided with capital sums, transferable – in

Property relations

the days before the Married Women's Property Act – to their husband on marriage. No woman in Austen thus appears as an active maker of money: the crucial economic activity of women was marriage, and through marriage access to the husband's income.[3]

A division of the sexes in terms of their access to property thus suggests a far more passive role in the economic world for women than for men. Women cannot – or do not – make money in Jane Austen, and their moral values about money are revealed in different ways from those of men. Women's morality about money is revealed, Austen suggests, largely through the extent to which they actively seek to marry for money, and regard money as a crucial consideration in the choice of their husband. Men's relationship to property is inevitably more complex, since it is more varied. The country estate is again crucial here, for Austen makes men's attitude to it one measure of male virtue and good judgement. But estates also have another importance in the way that they can bring together (or divorce) the understanding of men and women. For example, in *Pride and Prejudice*, Mr Darcy's estate – though geographically and socially distant from the Bennet home and the main events of the novel – is in a structural sense the most important place in the novel, for it is at Pemberley that Elizabeth Bennet sees for the first time that Darcy is no male dilettante but a man with a genuine – if hierarchically organized – concern for the lives of those people who depend on him. Mr Knightley's estate in *Emma* is, in the same way, to be Emma's spiritual and emotional home: although eventually Mr Knightley has to begin his married life in Mr Woodhouse's house, it is only because of the very 'strength, resolution and presence of mind' of Mr Knightley that the marriage can occur at all, and he has aptly demonstrated that strength of character in his care and cultivation of Donwell, an estate which he has, in a sense, been 'saving' for Emma as she grows from infancy to adolescence and maturity.

Emma and *Pride and Prejudice* both contain instances of

21

the way in which Jane Austen associates secure, well-tended, and well-cared-for country estates with male virtue. The process of the moral education of the heroines that occurs in these novels in part involves their recognition of the virtues of individual character that have made possible the prosperity and stability of Pemberley and Donwell Abbey. Both of these estates are prosperous, Jane Austen points out, not through an accident of nature, but because of the care, the attention, and the good judgement exercised by the owner. The housekeeper whom Elizabeth Bennet meets at Pemberley thus commends Mr Darcy: ' "He is the best landlord, and the best master," said she, "that ever lived. Not like the wild young men now-a-days, who think of nothing but themselves. There is not one of his tenants or servants but will give him a good name." '[4]

But access to these fine estates, and the world of their owners, is not to be given without a concession from the heroines, and what Emma and Elizabeth both have to abandon is a belief in the infallibility of their judgement. Elizabeth Bennet cannot become mistress of Pemberley, and an overseer of the Darcy inheritance, until she can be trusted to value the qualities that have made that inheritance possible. Educated – or perhaps mis-educated – by her father into the very accurate recognition of pomposity and dullness, Elizabeth has failed to recognize the possibility that liveliness and wit do not constitute virtue. Like other characters in Austen (most particularly Edmund Bertram in *Mansfield Park*) Elizabeth has to learn that those qualities which can guarantee the happiness and security of others are not necessarily those which are most immediately apparent in drawing-room conversation.

Emma's belief in her own judgement is as developed as that of Elizabeth Bennet, but more active. If we were to conjecture on the causes of this difference, it might be that the reason for Emma's greater interest in the manipulation of others arises not just from the greater material resources at her command but also from the experience of living with Mr Woodhouse, a man who has made inactivity into a career. If Emma is driven to meddle in the affairs of others the motive may be derived from frustration at her father's refusal to take any part in social life. Mr Bennet, on the other hand, though in a sense as inactive as Mr Woodhouse (as Mr Bennet seldom stirs from his study so Mr Woodhouse seldom stirs from his fireside), is nevertheless more actively engaged in the social world in his constant mockery of it and the activities of individuals within it. Both men have, of course, developed strategies for absence from social life: the one by satire and cynicism, the other by invalidism and learned incompetence. Both their daughters, on the other hand, show a marked inclination to take on the social world: Elizabeth Bennet is the most physically active of Jane Austen's heroines and Emma is by far the most socially interventionist. Deprived of active masculinity in their fathers, both these daughters more than adequately take on some of the masculine characteristics of sons.

So the liveliness, the vitality, and the energy of Elizabeth and Emma are, perhaps, the result of the inactivity of their fathers: people who are, after all, supposed to be positively involved in the affairs of the world. But as with all reactive characteristics – and hence the need for the moral re-education of Emma and Elizabeth – the energy of both is easily falsely directed. What the energy requires is proper organization by the solid patriarchal figures of Mr Knightley and Mr Darcy. Thus on an interpersonal level, the marriages of Emma and Mr Knightley, and Elizabeth and Mr Darcy, seem to be entirely appropriate: the women are, in a sense, tamed by the better judgement and the wider experience of the world of their husbands, whilst the men are given more levity by interaction with their lively wives. Hence in the concluding chapters of *Emma* Mr Knightley acquires a greater vivacity and certainly a less ponderous conversational tone than had previously been his, whilst Mr Darcy, in his final conversations with Elizabeth in *Pride and Prejudice*, speaks with greater *élan* and fluency than had previously been the case. Jane Austen leaves her readers in no doubt that these marriages will unite people who have lived through mutual misunderstanding, and who have acted – through misunderstanding – in ways which they will renounce.

In all, female impetuosity has been tempered by male judgement and women who could not admire their fathers have found in their husbands those virtues absent in the patriarch. The material equations of the marriages are not, of course, identical: Elizabeth takes nothing to Pemberley, Emma is independently wealthy. Yet if we consider what Mrs Knightley and Mrs Darcy do give to their husbands – in a metaphorical rather than a personal sense – we will find that what they are taking to the ancestral estates is a spirit which will give them a justification for existence. However carefully tended Pemberley and Donwell Abbey might be, they are not, in the absence of heirs and a set of social relationships, *living* estates. The liveliness of Elizabeth and Emma is such that it suggests a continuity of existence: whatever the 'culture' of Donwell and Pemberley they are nothing without the 'nature' of lively women. Property, therefore, is given a meaning through the appropriation by men of the energies of women.

In *Emma* and *Pride and Prejudice* the central estate of the novel is – as we have seen – a well-arranged one, that only needs the appropriate mistress to make it into a wholly integrated community. In the other novels it is more often that the estates are mismanaged, and either need reparation by a female hand or involve the exile of a heroine. Mansfield Park is far from a mismanaged estate in the literal, material sense, but it is crucially mismanaged morally: in an interesting parallel, just as Austen ensures the continued existence of Pemberley and Donwell by the character of their new mistresses, so she in part suggests the potential – and eventual – structural weakness of Mansfield Park through the vapid, empty presence of Lady Bertram. A series of 'ifs' thus emerges in *Mansfield Park* about the relationship of women to property – if Lady Bertram had been more actively and positively involved in the education of her daughters, then matchmaking on their behalf might not have been left to the dubious judgement of Mrs Norris. Equally, if Sir Thomas Bertram had not given such a high priority to the appearance of his estate (in the sense of the absolute maintenance by all its members of rigid, formal codes of behaviour) then his daughter Maria might not have been so tempted by the appearance of Mr Rushworth's estate and property – a considerable wealth that was empty of either talent or intelligence.

But Lady Bertram was not inclined to take any part in the activities of her daughters and Maria Bertram was tempted by the wealth of Mr Rushworth. In this temptation it is possible to see an individual who parodies the values of a person they dislike: Maria, who dislikes her father and his values, makes a mockery of him and his apparent interests by the marriage to Rushworth. Existing as she has to, under patriarchal authority and constraint, it is an act of defiance to marry Rushworth – to say to the constraining father that this is the human embodiment of his apparent values and to make of that human being an albatross for the parent. This act of revolt is, for Maria, the act that ruins her, for she can no more tolerate Mr Rushworth than can her father, and in her rejection of Rushworth and flight with Henry Crawford she lives to humiliate her father, and exile herself for ever from the community at Mansfield Park. The rot in the estate has worked itself out – and Mansfield Park is only saved by the presence of Fanny Price, the angel in the house who eventually becomes the moral centre of Sir Thomas's estate. A woman, as in *Emma* and *Pride and Prejudice*, is produced to give certainty to the property of men. The Victorian hymn which ends with the lines 'speak through the earthquake, fire and storm, O still small voice of calm', summarizes the place of Fanny Price in the turmoil of events at Mansfield Park in the conclusion to the novel. Other people – men – rush about, write letters, travel to London, and generally engage in frantic activity in order to repair the damage of Maria's adulterous elopement, Julia's marriage, and Tom's profligacy: all these energetic activities have nothing like the same efficacy as the return to Mansfield of the slight figure of Fanny. It is an event which – uncharacteristically – provokes Lady Bertram to leave her sofa and to say to Fanny, 'Dear Fanny! now I shall be comfortable.'[5]

When Fanny returns to Mansfield Park she brings with her the promise of a reorganized community, one which values more than formally correct behaviour. If we read *Mansfield Park* as a metaphor for English society (and it is tempting to do so, since it is Jane Austen's most enclosed novel), we find that she suggests to us that a society cannot live only through the observation by its citizens of formal rules and regulations – those legalistic, or quasi-legalistic, restraints on their behaviour have to have a basis in morality of concern for others and a community of values. To force, or constrain, individuals to act in certain ways is to ensure the kind of delinquency that manifests itself in the Bertram sisters – desperate behaviour that is born out of a desperate sense of constraint. The violence of the reaction of Maria and Julia (and they rebel far more actively than other Austen characters) is therefore a measure of the sense of frustration that both have endured for years. Too much constraint, Austen suggests, is therefore likely to lead to evil, to truly reprehensible behaviour – whereas too little constraint (as in the case of Lydia Bennet in *Pride and Prejudice*) leads to folly, rather than what Austen might describe as vice. The perception by Sir Thomas that he can only safeguard his property, and indeed his world, through formal legislation, rigid rules, and constant surveillance is – if reproduced by a society – a perception that will only lead to precisely the kind of behaviour that its constraints are designed to eliminate.

Mansfield Park is in many ways Austen's most fully ideological novel, in that she sets out in it with almost evangelical clarity her views on the proper organization of society. But in the context of a discussion of property relations, it must also be observed that it is the novel in which she comes closest to suggesting an alliance, in ideological terms, between those with property and those without. What she is in effect saying, therefore, in *Mansfield Park* is that no community, however rich or prosperous, can prosper or survive without a secure moral basis and that morality is not derived from property, or from the relationships of property. Indeed, the relationships of property in the novel – those between Maria and Mr Rushworth, Sir Thomas and his dependants (in that he regards them as part of his property and therefore subject to his absolute control) – are those which are most doomed to fail. Self-interested self-aggrandisement (the temptation to marry his daughter to a wealthy man, 'a marriage which would bring him such an addition of respectability and influence', and the further possibility of a match between his niece and Henry Crawford) is Sir Thomas's moral flaw: the enlargement of his world is a seductive possibility, and he is, at first, unable to ask critical questions about the need or the fitness of acquiring new territories for his patriarchal influence. The temptations of property, Austen is suggesting, are therefore many: individuals do not merely wish to maintain their property, they also wish to enlarge it, and they are prepared to sacrifice the interests of individuals in order to do so. Readers are left in no doubt that Sir Thomas recognizes Rushworth as a stupid young man, and that Fanny is indeed attracted to Henry Crawford. But people, and human happiness, are not concerns which patriarchal capitalism takes seriously: just as the Harlowes would happily sacrifice Clarissa to Lovelace to enrich themselves, so Sir Thomas is content to give other interests precedence over the personal happiness of Fanny and Maria.

Property and wealth can therefore be a trap, a cause of unhappiness and dissent. In *Mansfield Park* the correction to the prioritization of property comes from Fanny, a person who, entirely alone and literally penniless, confronts the wealth and the power of Sir Thomas. In fiction it is an encounter from which Fanny emerges victorious, in the sense that it is her values and her judgement which will prove to be correct. But in reality, in the real social world of inequalities of wealth and power, it is difficult to see how the same influence could be brought to bear on arbitrary power. Thus when Austen suggests in *Mansfield Park* that wealth and the wealthy are not necessarily good, and that only a community with a moral sense can survive, she still leaves outstanding the issue of how, in reality, wealth and power are to be constrained and limited. It is comforting to read in *Mansfield Park* of the vindication of a heroine who has had a difficult childhood and adolescence, but the real world might not so conveniently provide an Edmund Bertram to reward Fanny for her faithfulness and tenacity. However, the moral message of the novel is not one that is concerned with reality and fantasy: the substance of Austen's message is the more substantial suggestion that wealth, the pursuit of property, and a developed fondness for it do not constitute virtue. Here, then, is the potentially radical message of *Mansfield Park*: the ownership of property is not in any sense a guide to the moral worth of the individual.

This message challenges one of the central tenets of capitalist thinking both in the early nineteenth and the late twentieth centuries, that material and moral prosperity are synonymous. Although the belief has, at specific points in British history such as wartime, been rejected, it is still very much the case that it is constantly necessary to demonstrate that the poor are poor through the circumstances of the material and social world and not through their individual failings or shortcomings. The belief in the possibility of each and every citizen to be prosperous within the existing relations of capitalist production is one that not only dies hard, but shows no sign of even the beginning of a terminal illness. Indeed, at the present time the policies of the British Conservative Party positively endorse the belief that people's poverty is in some way related to their moral capabilities. The message of *Mansfield Park* is deeply disturbing for those who hold this view: the rich demonstrate not only their capacity for vice, but the poor demonstrate their capacity for virtue. According to the calculating ethic of self-interest promoted by the champions of the market economy of sexual relations, Fanny should have (indeed, would have) married Henry Crawford: how could such a match have been resisted? When Jane Austen remarked that she had, in Fanny Price, created a character who would not be liked by everyone, she meant, perhaps, that many people would find Fanny Price difficult to accept precisely because of her capacity, that few people share, for absolute resistance to capitalist values. Of all the Austen characters, Fanny Price has a complete integrity of purpose, an integrity which is a direct challenge to notions of personal self-enhancement or enrichment. With consummate skill, Austen teases her readers into supposing that Henry Crawford is not, perhaps, such an unacceptable man after all: perhaps, she artfully suggests, we should overlook Henry's flirtation with Maria or his cold-blooded decision to amuse himself by 'making a small hole in Fanny Price's heart'.[6] As Henry Crawford sets out to make himself a more attractive man, so he gradually becomes more considerate and more apparently committed. He survives the rigours of a meeting with the Price family with credit, and is looking more and more morally creditable when an idle inclination encourages him to stay in London. There, of course, he meets Maria Bertram again, and just as the maintenance of his wealth and social position is Sir Thomas's fatal weakness, so the exercise of his sexual powers is Henry Crawford's. Tempted once again to demonstrate to himself the powers of his sexual attractiveness, he finds himself involved in a situation which eventually guarantees his exile from Fanny for ever.

So it emerges that Fanny was right in her judgement of Henry Crawford: vanity has an organizing force in his character and it is a vanity which plays havoc with the lives of others. But the one person whose life is unaffected by this failing is Fanny Price; precisely because she is disinclined to value either property or socially constructed concepts of sexual and personal charm, she is untouched by the consequences of living out the pursuit of these seductions. Henry Crawford represents therefore the temptations of both money and sexuality: his estate is substantial, and his charm, in the sense that it is conventionally understood by characters other than Fanny, is considerable. Given the extent of Fanny's resistance to convention, it is small wonder that Jane Austen expected few readers to like her; even less would they like the author's articulation of a deep suspicion of many apparently engaging and amusing aspects of social life. Yet Fanny – both poor and female – overturns the values of Mansfield Park, and has by the end of the novel succeeded in making the majority of the characters look either ridiculous, evil, or unreliable in their judgement. Perhaps no character in fiction offers such a radical critique of bourgeois patriarchy, its norms, and values of behaviour, as Fanny Price, a woman who does not end the novel dead like Clarissa, but alive, well, and valued.

The limits of the social and physical space of *Mansfield Park* make possible the very thorough examination of the motives and actions of its central characters. The pressures of intimate family life are vividly described; apparently spacious and gracious, life at Mansfield Park is in fact closely circumscribed by a rigid code of behaviour. The inadequacies of this code for dealing with human passions and inclinations are fully described by Jane Austen, but she also shows that in part the code enforced by Sir Thomas represses real needs to such an extent that they appear in distorted forms: because Julia and Maria have never been taught anything but the manners of genteel society they have no capacity to recognize the realities of stupidity and folly. The paradox of Fanny's difference from Julia and Maria is that although apparently the most sheltered and circumscribed of the three, it is in fact she who can recognize selfishness, vanity, and lack of consideration for others. Julia and Maria, in their greater sophistication and worldliness, have lost or have never developed the ability to see individuals in other than social terms. Using an index of social manners – which measures appearance, wit, and charm and is uninterested in the ways in which individuals behave towards each other – the Bertram sisters evaluate people in superficial terms. Both of them represent that perception of individuals which takes the values of the market-place (both sexual and material) and accepts them as the only values of human existence.

So to the world of fashion and success Jane Austen demonstrates an implacable resistance. Which is not to say that she is not as capable as any other educated person of recognizing charm, beauty, and taste: the distinction between her recognition of these qualities and that of the Bertram sisters is that she recognizes them as created, learned capacities. Money, she realizes, can buy taste, charm, and the appearance of education. Wealth does, of course, have its spectacular failures, in that no amount of money can transform Mr Rushworth into anything other than a very stupid, dull young man, but equally the balance sheet of her novels suggests that Jane Austen is inclined to conclude that the possession of wealth can give human beings the appearance, albeit sometimes false, of charm and personal attractiveness. Throughout the novels Austen creates characters – most frequently men – who can make themselves appear attractive through the purchase of the means of personal ostentation and appropriately masculine behaviour. Tom Bertram is 'dashing' – not because of any innate qualities, but because, in common with other young men of his class, he can afford to ride around on expensive horses. Marianne, in *Sense and Sensibility*, is charmed by Willoughby's appearance and his smart carriage. The glamour and the seductive vision of herself that Marianne constructs from this vehicle, and a brief acquaintance with its owner, are very nearly responsible for her death. Disappointed in what she had regarded as a perfect love, Marianne almost succumbs to a fever. Physical objects and physical appearance are thus suggested as the fantasies that can frequently deceive: or if deceive is too strong a term, then at least promise more than is actually to be found. 'All that glitters is not gold', 'beauty is only skin deep' are not the sentiments that Jane Austen is expressing: her message is more complex than a simple suspicion of wealth (although that is certainly an element in her argument). Rather than suspicion therefore, she is suggesting that we should examine very carefully the ways in which we regard the possibilities of human action and creation. Yes: people can create vast wealth, exhibit astonishing beauty and physical prowess, but the question then to be asked – and to be asked most urgently in a society in which the creation of vast wealth appears an immediate possibility – is how we evaluate these possibilities in moral terms. What, in short, should people with moral and ethical concerns and values do – and think – about money?

It is apparent, from *Northanger Abbey* to *Persuasion*, that Jane Austen never alters her basic and fundamental belief in the inadequacy of relating the possession of money to the possession of virtue. But this position is, of course, hardly adequate to the description and the understanding of social life; what is more central to Austen's concerns is an examination of the ways in which the possession of money, or lack of it, structures and organizes human motivation. Some characters in her fiction are, as we have seen, both rich and 'good' in a quite straightforward sense of the term. Mr Darcy, Colonel Brandon, and Mr Knightley are, therefore, honest, kind, and scrupulously honourable in their dealings with other people: they do not lie, dissemble, or flirt with women (whether married or unmarried), and they exercise a consistent loyalty to their families and their dependants. As models of behaviour they therefore represent all those characteristics which Austen obviously values. Equally, just as Mr Darcy, Colonel Brandon, and Mr Knightley are straightforwardly rich and good, so Lady Catherine de Bourgh, Mrs John Dashwood, and Mrs Ferrars are rich and unpleasant. Not actually evil in any deeply destructive sense, but, at the very least, biased, rude, and prejudiced. In *Northanger Abbey*, *Sense and Sensibility*, *Pride and Prejudice*, and *Emma* we therefore have both the good, and less good, rich. We also have – in the forms of Willoughby and Wickham – men who are inconsiderate and selfish in their treatment of others, and who act badly largely on account of material greed. But in case we should suppose that it is only men who are materially greedy, Jane Austen offers us, in *Sense and Sensibility*, the person of Lucy Steele, a female adventurer in the tradition of Moll Flanders.

These characters, however, represent cases of clear motivation and straightforward perception – whether right or wrong, selfish or otherwise. The more complex cases, and in an important sense the forerunners of the more thorough investigation of the relationship between property and virtue in *Mansfield Park* and *Persuasion*, are Mr Bennet, Charlotte Lucas, and Emma herself. All these characters, in one way or another, pose interesting moral questions in terms of the way in which they deal with the material world. They are not selfish in the same way as Willoughby or Wickham; equally Jane Austen suggests to us that the way that they regard the material world is a very good guide to their character. Mr Bennet, clever, well-read, and witty, is therefore lazy and indolent in his attitude to property: disinclined to pay any serious attention to his estate, he has created a situation in which his wife and daughters face poverty on his death. Charlotte Lucas, in the same novel, is prepared to endure a lifetime with Mr Collins in order to secure for herself material provision. Her obvious and admitted reservations about Mr Collins therefore pale into nothing compared to the evaluation of his worth as a material provider. And finally Emma herself, rich and self-assured, but inclined to waste her talents and energies on idle matchmaking and dilettantish attempts at sketching and music. Mr Bennet and Emma therefore suggest the possibilities of the waste of resources – whilst Charlotte Lucas suggests an attitude of cynical calculation.

Jane Austen and the State

The puzzle, and the interest, of all these cases, is how these characters come to act as they do. Is Mr Bennet actually indolent, or is the task of amassing a small surplus actually impossible? Is Charlotte Lucas just enough like Mr Collins to endure life with him? And is Emma, without the guiding hand of Mr Knightley, the thoughtless heiress that her behaviour sometimes suggests? In these novels, the central events occur too quickly for us to assess the reasons for the characters' behaviour: there is – unlike in *Mansfield Park* and *Persuasion* – no alteration in the material circumstances of the characters and hence no insight into how they might behave in the light of different situations. The Dashwood sisters, like the Bennet sisters, enter the novel poor, and – like them – are redeemed at the end by men, and men's fortunes. But in *Mansfield Park* and *Persuasion* material life has a greater instability: what is suggested in these two novels, unlike the others, is structural instability in material life, rather than material difficulties arising from personal circumstances. Mansfield Park – unlike Pemberley and Donwell Abbey – is thus a threatened estate: it is difficulties at the estates in the West Indies that remove Sir Thomas from his rightful place as head of the household. No such difficulties confront Darcy or Mr Knightley. The security of the life of the landowner is, in both cases, absolute, and Mr Darcy can leave home in the perfect security that his income will continue. Mr Knightley, it is true, seldom leaves home, but this is less due to concern for his estate than personal taste. But the continuum of material security along which Jane Austen's novels move reaches the extreme of banishment from the estate in *Persuasion*, her final novel. Here, the idle and extravagant Sir Walter Elliot has so conspicuously failed to make his estate pay that he is forced to go and live in furnished rooms in Bath, an unhappy exile with only tenuous aristocratic connections to console him for the loss of his property.

The years between the publication of *Pride and Prejudice*, *Sense and Sensibility*, *Emma*, and *Northanger Abbey* on the one hand, and *Persuasion* and *Mansfield Park* on the other, cover a period in English history in which the livelihood of the gentry, and the aristocratic landowner, became more materially problematic. As already suggested, all Austen's novels (with the exception of *Northanger Abbey*) carry hints of the world outside that of the materially secure. But only in *Mansfield Park* and *Persuasion* do we see middle-aged men forced to include material questions and problems in their calculations. What this suggests is a world of changing economic patterns: the men who have to make their fortunes, by fair means or foul, in *Pride and Prejudice*, *Emma*, and *Sense and Sensibility*, are all young: the middle-aged, the married, the socially established all have a place in the material world that is apparently secure. But not so for Sir Thomas and Sir Walter: their worlds are threatened, and an established order of patriarchal figures is under attack. Indeed, what begins to occur in *Mansfield Park* and *Persuasion* is a separation of the moral and the material qualities of individuals, an increasing recognition that the greatest security for human beings lies in their personal qualities and not in their material circumstances. Thus we are assured that William Price will make his way in the world because of his application and his integrity; in the same way Captain Wentworth, in *Persuasion*, has made his way through conscientious commitment to his profession.

So what emerges in the late Austen novels is an entirely self-made, morally admirable hero. The message to the decadent Tom Bertram and Sir Walter Elliot is clear: your world will not be maintained through behaviour that is careless and arrogant, a new code of values has to be evolved for the propertied in order for that property to be maintained. Even more important perhaps, Jane Austen asks us to consider the value of maintaining the worlds of Sir Thomas and Sir Walter: the world of Sir Thomas is repressive and over-formal, that of Sir Walter silly and vain. The mistake of Anne Elliot – in initially refusing Captain Wentworth because of his apparent lack of standing in the world of the country gentry – is a mistake which Austen demonstrates as arising from a too conservative commitment to an outmoded set of priorities about a vanished world. Aristocratic titles (the baronetcy so dear to Sir Walter's heart) and formal manners are shown as a barrier to the existence, and the development, of human happiness. The blindness of Elizabeth Elliot to the lack of interest of Admiral and Mrs Croft in her invitations is a vivid representation of the potential failure of a redundant aristocracy to perceive their irrelevance to a world changing in both its material and its social relationships.

By the time *Persuasion* was published in 1818 it must have become apparent to an astute observer of the social world that radical changes were occurring in the organization of social and economic life. For the gentry, the crucial change was the increased commercialization of agriculture. Men who did not regard their estates as commercial ventures were less and less able to remain financially viable. Hence to regard a country estate primarily as a source of status (as did Sir Walter Elliot) was to commit economic suicide: in a capitalist society all assets have to be regarded as material and exploitable. And included among the assets of the world that are to be exploited are human beings themselves: exploitable not only in the sense that the maximum labour should be extracted from them, but in the sense that it is a primary duty of human beings to contribute to the social world. For some critics of Austen's work, notably Marilyn Butler and Alistair Duckworth, this places her firmly in a tradition of conservative values: both see Austen as arguing that a properly organized moral sense can, if integrated into a traditional community (be it a family or an estate), save it from corruption and decay. Duckworth emphasizes the importance Austen places on attitudes to estates and their management by individual characters: the 'good' manage their estates properly, the 'bad' are uninterested landlords. Marilyn Butler, in sharing Duckworth's view of Austen as conservative, suggests that a further – and crucial – element in Austen's world view is her suspicion of individualism.

Property relations

Associating this with Austen's anti-Jacobin sentiments, Butler argues that Austen is profoundly suspicious of individual inclination that is not tempered by social and moral values; concluding her discussion Butler writes:

> 'Jane Austen's novels contain central characters more given to rejection than fictional heroes and heroines of the first part of the century, and she makes it clear how much she values the probings of the rational moral intelligence. . . . Her plots are a movement from ignorance to knowledge, culminating in a moment of intelligent discernment, and this in itself is bi-partisan.'
>
> (Butler 1975: 293)

And Butler continues: 'The plots of Jane Austen's novels begin in the conservative camp and, very significantly, remain in it.'

In identifying Jane Austen with the anti-Jacobin movement of the late eighteenth century Marilyn Butler contributes enormously to scholarship on the author by demonstrating that she is far from removed from the ideological debates and disputes of her day. Yet what still needs to be explained in the work of both Marilyn Butler and Alistair Duckworth, is why Austen's perception of the dangers of romance and intuition – and her care for the stability of human relationships and communities – should be regarded as conservative.

In assessing the reasons why Austen is regarded as conservative and deeply traditional, two emerge as particularly important. The first is that Austen is generally regarded as seeing urban life as morally suspect; thus Butler writes that Mary Crawford has been given 'selfish values' by urban life (1975: 224). In this same vein we can cite those other examples in Austen which seem to associate city life (and particularly London life) with frivolity and corruption: Frank Churchill goes to London to get his hair cut, it is in London that Willoughby so publicly and callously rejects Marriane, and it is in Bath that Sir Walter Elliot finds the parties and assemblies at which to play his silly social games. But against these examples we must also set those of Mr and Mrs Gardiner, a couple who live in London (indeed, in sight of their 'own warehouses') and yet are models of good sense and courteous manners, whilst it is in Bath that Captain Wentworth and Anne Elliot recognize their still strong affections. There is, therefore, no absolute connection in Austen between cities and vice, and the country and virtue. Characters who are corrupt remain as such whether in the town or the country.

But to twentieth-century eyes it can appear that Austen is praising the life of the countryside as in some sense morally superior to that of the town, and thus apparently endorsing 'traditional' life over that of a more modern form of society. The point here, however, is that for Jane Austen – unlike her twentieth-century readers – the country was typical rather than traditional: few people lived in large urban areas and the general experience of community life was that of a small village. Austen's objection to the city – if that is as substantial as is sometimes suggested – is therefore that it allowed more possibility for unchecked folly than did a small community. It is not then city life *per se* – in terms of the occupations of people within the city – that Austen suspects, but the loss in large-scale, relatively anonymous communities of people's better judgement and better sense. The temptation of the city is that of undefined and unstructured social space: the space which suggests to individuals that there is a possibility of living out, without notice or constraint, their more dubious inclinations. Writing of Paris in the nineteenth century Walter Benjamin observed that it was in the city that people could live out their fantasies: they could escape notice and yet at the same time they could also receive recognition without judgement (1973: 157–76). Much the same view is echoed by characters in Austen: city life provokes all the female characters into a flurry of clothes buying and anxious attention to dress – here at last is an audience to satisfy narcissism. It is clear that Austen regards this as harmless (her own letters show that as soon as she set foot in London and Bath she engaged in much the same exercise) but what she does not regard as harmless is the excessive value which some characters attach to the range of possibilities offered by towns. Thus the major point of her critique of urban life is not that towns are inherently immoral, rather that urban life can allow the silly, or the morally corrupt, to articulate and demonstrate more fully the range and depth of their cupidity. To those with the kind of values that Austen endorses the city offers no threat: the city may be dirty and noisy and the glare from the buildings oppressive (as Austen herself found was the case in Bath) but it is not in itself a cause of corruption.

So Austen's view of the city is more complex than that of the simple-minded conservative who regards the mere sight of the countryside as in some sense morally uplifting. To suspect the values that can be encouraged in conditions of anonymity and the pursuit of fashion is, perhaps, not so much conservative as radical: to ask questions, in the context of capitalist social relations, about exactly what is being valued and lauded by leaders of fashion and arbiters of taste is to ask questions about conspicuous consumption, false distinctions, and misleading constructions of individuality. Although *Northanger Abbey* is Austen's most imperfectly realized novel, it does contain a vivid hint of her suspicion of the hold of fashion and the dream of a fashionable appearance on young girls. Thus Catherine Morland's chaperone in Bath, Mrs Allen, is described:

'The air of a gentlewoman, a great deal of quiet, inactive good temper, and a trifling turn of mind were all that could account for her being the choice of a sensible, intelligent man like Mr. Allen. . . . Dress was her passion. . . . Mrs. Allen was so long in dressing that they did not enter the ballroom till late. . . . With more care for the safety of her new gown than for the comfort of her protégée, Mrs. Allen made her way through the throng of men by the door.'[7]

A sense of priorities is established here, harmless enough in this case but possibly deeply damaging in others.

Those other cases are Maria Bertram, Mrs Elton, and Lucy Steele: women for whom what is an innocent enjoyment in dress in Mrs Allen becomes a strong desire for the means of its purchase (in the case of Maria Bertram and Lucy Steele) or the means of judging others (in the case of Mrs Elton). Fashion and appearance are thus seductive – and for some individuals, irresistible. This suspicion of an overdeveloped interest in appearance leads to a second theme in Austen which has been regarded as an instance of her conservatism – her suspicion of romanticism and individualistic expressions of sentiment and passion. Again, it is appropriate to question the presumption that this suspicion is conservative rather than radical, and inhibiting rather than liberating. In those passages in *Sense and Sensibility* in which Marianne Dashwood enthuses most energetically about the countryside, it is possible to see the forerunner of the twentieth-century romantic adolescent (or indeed individual of any age) who will repeatedly fail to recognize either the reality of his or her own needs or the possibility that other people will create artificial desires. When Edward Ferrars remarks that he would 'call hills steep, which ought to be bold; surfaces strange and uncouth, which ought to be irregular and rugged'[8] he is speaking for accuracy and veracity in speech and representation. Against the unbridled romanticism of Mariane, Edward is maintaining that it is possible to describe the physical world in precise and objective terms.

As *Sense and Sensibility* unfolds it is clear that Jane Austen is developing a sustained and coherent attack upon fantasies of romance and visions of transcendent relationships between men and women. The semi-fantastical figure of Willoughby who emerges out of the woods to rescue Marianne is a figure who eventually reveals himself to have been created by Marianne's dreams and romantic aspirations: the 'real' Willoughby, in the sense of the specific human being who enters into specific social and sexual relationships with others, is a callous and inadequate adventurer. The 'real' feeling which Marianne sees in Willoughby is little except his need to demonstrate sexual power over women, and it is a power in part created by her own need for romance and identification with a male other. Hence it is precisely Marianne's lack of genuine autonomy or sense of self that encourages her to project fantasy on to Willoughby – a projection that elicits from Willoughby the living out, in the isolation of the Devon countryside, the dream of the romantic hero.

That dream cannot be sustained in the real world of social – and particularly material – relationships, for neither Willoughby nor Marianne has an income sufficient to maintain themselves in marriage. The fantasies that the pair have created thus prove entirely inadequate for a sustained relationship. The intimacy which both had believed existed was one which did not include the intimacy of shared responsibility or shared commitment – it was an intimacy of feeling, and of a particular kind of romantic feeling that Jane Austen suggests to us is deeply problematic in the real world. But to label this suspicion of romanticism and fantasy as conservative is perhaps questionable, for far from endorsing the sentiments, and the organization of sentiment, in capitalist society, Jane Austen is surely questioning it, in that she is asking us to examine critically those emotional states which we label as 'love', and 'need', and 'passion'. That strong affections exist between human beings she accepts, and indeed endorses, but what she is questioning is the development, in the late eighteenth century, of ideologies of romance and transcendence in individual relationships. The fully developed characters in Austen's fiction are not, therefore, those who 'need' others in a desperate sense; they are already able to live in a certain harmony both with themselves and with others.

That romance is a trap for both men and women is a message which Austen repeatedly suggests. But more than that, she questions the individualization of feeling that was

41

emerging in the earliest years of industrial capitalism and has remained ever since. She therefore asks her characters to look less at their specific individuality than at their generality: it is far more important, she argues, that people recognize the needs that all share – for material provision, social recognition, commitment, and the means to support their children – than individualize need by romance or fantasy. Jane Austen's detached observation of the social world clearly led her to conclude that the recognition of material and emotional need was too often distorted, and indeed obscured, by socially created ideologies. Nearly 200 years of the burgeoning of the industries of romance, sexual titillation, and pornographic representations of sexuality suggest that the very same relationships of property which existed in Jane Austen's day have developed an increased capacity to obscure many of the realities of both the material and the emotional needs of individuals. The fantasy figure of Willoughby is a forerunner of the sexual hero of late capitalism – a man created and endorsed by precisely those conservative – and patriarchal – interests which Jane Austen challenges.

3
Questioning the patriarchal order

For many contemporary feminists Jane Austen's novels have neither interest nor a place in a feminist tradition. It is enough to note that Austen accepts heterosexual marriage for her to be condemned and crossed off the list of feminism's leading figures. Nevertheless, other discussions of Jane Austen and feminism have been less dismissive. For example, Margaret Kirkham has argued that: 'Jane Austen's heroines are not self-conscious feminists, yet they are all exemplary of the first claim of Enlightenment feminism: that women share the same moral nature as men, ought to share the same moral status, and exercise the same responsibility for their own conduct.' (1983: 84).

Those claims – for women and men to be regarded as moral equals and allowed equal responsibility for their conduct – challenge many of the assumptions that have emerged since the late eighteenth century: that moral rules should be different for men and women and that women (like children) do not have the capacity to make viable moral choices. Both beliefs have been articulated through the practices and the laws of the British state – the Contagious Diseases Act of 1867 is the most notorious example of nineteenth-century legislation which attempted to enshrine the principle of the sexual double standard. Throughout the nineteenth and twentieth centuries, women's adultery has generally been seen as more culpable than men's. In contested divorce cases, women's extramarital sexual relations have often been interpreted and condemned with greater severity than men's.

43

Jane Austen and the State

The catalogue of instances in which the state has enforced the sexual double standard is now extensive, well researched, and well documented. Jane Austen's world contained relatively little specific legislation on sexuality and morality, but situations of course arose in which judgements about individual behaviour had to be made. Austen's thesis is consistent with the principle of moral equality between the sexes: men and women must, and should, act according to the same values, and the misbehaviour of one sex is no excuse or reason for the misbehaviour of the other. This principle of a single standard of sexual morality pre-dates the Enlightenment (although Margaret Kirkham rightly emphasizes its place in Enlightenment feminism) and represents a consistent – and consistently challenged – tradition within the history of English morality. As Christopher Hill has argued, in an essay on *Clarissa*, 'Clarissa travelled, if this is not too fanciful, through the whole history of humanity. . . . She passed through and revolted against the feudal-patriarchal family and the tyranny of money; she looked forward to a society in which women shall have attained full equality of status' (1968: 376).

An essential ingredient of Austen's feminism is, therefore, that she upholds with great vigour that tradition within English morality which condemns the sexual, indeed the moral, double standard.

But Austen can be interpreted as a feminist, I would argue, for two reasons other than that of her support for an existing moral tradition. First, Austen values the part that women play in domestic and family life, and second, she portrays women as acting, and capable of acting, independently of men and patriarchal interests. Austen's morality then is one which does not endorse worldly self-interest, public and fashionable standards, material self-enhancement, or entrepreneurial greed. It is a moot point, not to be discussed here, whether these attitudes and standards should be associated essentially with men, on the grounds that an inclination to accumulate material profit and public power and status is a male rather than a female attribute. What can be said in this context, however, is that – for whatever reason – it is men, rather than women, who are engaged in and associated with the public world – and hence more likely to be compromised or challenged by its demands. Even so, Austen points out in all her novels that even if it is men who are more actively engaged in the public world, it is entirely incorrect to assume from this that women have neither an interest in, nor an influence over, those vexed questions of the capitalist world of profit and loss, gain and accumulation, and status and hierarchy. Women, she emphasizes (perhaps to the discomfort of those contemporary feminists who would like to see women as living in a morally separate world from that of men), do not inhabit a distinctive social or moral universe.

In arguing for a feminist reading of Jane Austen, the first characteristic of her work which I would emphasize is that she portrays women as moral adults, and moral adults in one particularly important sense for feminists, namely that amongst her female characters are those women who choose or countenance the possibility of living without men and male approval, rather than compromise central principles of behaviour. Although Austen's accounts of marriages suggest that many are less than perfectly happy she does nevertheless show that – to paraphrase the feminist slogan – there is both a life after marriage (in, for example, the case of Mr and Mrs Gardiner, Admiral and Mrs Croft, Mr and Mrs Weston, *et al.*) and a life without marriage (a possibility entertained by Elinor Dashwood, Anne Elliot, *et al.*). Elinor Dashwood, Jane and Elizabeth Bennet, Anne Elliot, and Fanny Price are all women who would rather live unmarried than enter into marriage solely in response to the assumption of society that for women this is the only viable existence. In all the cases cited above the choice is neither simple nor attractive. Elinor Dashwood and the others are not choosing between marriage and a career or between independence and dependence in any contemporary sense. For all of them remaining single means remaining confined and largely penniless, dependent on parents or relatives, and with few prospects of a life of anything other than quiet seclusion. Their fate, indeed, would be that of Miss Bates in *Emma*. In one character Jane Austen portrays the possible future of many of her heroines, and vividly represents the point which many social historians have made: that marriage, in the eighteenth and nineteenth centuries, was an economic necessity for women. Far from being a matter of romantic or personal choice, the constraint on women to marry was very considerable.

But negotiating the terms of marriage has always been of crucial importance to women, and in her novels Austen makes two steps towards what we might describe as a modern feminist view of marriage: she questions, indeed pours scorn on, 'romance' and points out over and over again that marriage is a social and material contract. Unlike many of her contemporaries Austen had little time for romantic views of marriage or for romantic love between the sexes. The best example of this view is her satire on the Gothic novel, *Northanger Abbey*. Numerous passages in this novel suggest that the heroine could easily become a victim to highly questionable and indeed dangerous ideals of romance and the dramatic revelation of love. Thus,

> 'from fifteen to seventeen she was in training for a heroine; she read all such works as heroines must read to supply their memories with those quotations which are so serviceable and so soothing in the vicissitudes of their eventful lives. . . . And that a young woman in love always looks "like Patience on a monument smiling at grief".'[1]

Equipped with those vague, but deeply suggestive notions about the proper behaviour of women in love, the young Catherine sets off to Bath:

> 'Everything indeed relative to this important journey was done, on the part of the Morlands, with a degree of moderation and composure, which seemed rather consistent with the common feelings of common life, than with the refined susceptibilities, the tender emotions which the

first separation of a heroine from her family ought always to excite. Her father, instead of giving her an unlimited order to his banker, or even putting an hundred pounds bank-bill into her hands, gave her only ten guineas and promised her more when she wanted it.'[2]

In the passages above Austen demolishes the romantic expectations that might have filled Catherine Morland's head to the exclusion of all else, had she not been brought up in a large family in which romance had been specifically, and empirically, curtailed by reality. As it is, of course, Catherine is far from able to escape all romantic fantasy: Henry Tilney's home is full of false secrets and its very domesticity is invested by Catherine with vivid, and false, expectations. Austen is telling us that here is a potentially very silly young girl, encouraged by sillier novels and ridiculous ideas, who almost misinterprets the world to her own severe disadvantage.

The theme of the attack on romance, and romantic love as the basis for marriage, is to be found throughout Austen's work. *Northanger Abbey* takes the theme as its central concern, but the other novels all contain examples of the development of the same thesis: that fantasies about Mr Right, about dashing heroes, about the salvation of individuals – be they male or female – through a vision of transcendent heterosexual love are all false and dangerous. We are shown this through the example of couples who have married on the basis of sexual attraction: Mr and Mrs Bennet in *Pride and Prejudice* exemplify the couple who live a life of ill-matched discontent as a result of the fleeting passions of youth. But like father, so, in this case, like daughter, for Lydia Bennet, on the basis of a brief friendship, fancies herself in love with a worthless and deceitful young man. In a brilliant passage Austen describes Lydia Bennet's feelings for her husband:

'Lydia was exceedingly fond of him. He was her dear Wickham on every occasion; no one was to be put in competition with him. He did every thing best in the world;

and she was sure he would kill more birds on the first of September, than anybody else in the country.'[3]

Contemporary examples of Lydia Bennet walk the streets of every town and village in the world, adolescent girls whose heads have been subject to a barrage of romantic fiction and the endlessly hopeful lyrics of pop songs. 'Love and marriage go together like a horse and carriage' sang Doris Day in the 1950s and even if this sentiment is expressed less frequently in the popular ballads of the 1970s and 1980s, the same doe-eyed heroines of the teenage comics and magazines still wait miserably either for their acne to heal or for Mr Right to realize that their competitor for his affection is not really a very nice girl at all. Feminists throughout the west have attacked this culture and the expectations and aspirations that it creates: but all the evidence suggests that adolescent girls are still impressed, if not by the number of grouse that their suitors shoot, then at least by their masculine bravura in other areas.

But nearly 200 years before such critics of the teeny-bopper culture as McRobbie (1978), Cowie and Lees (1981), and Hudson (1984), Jane Austen was pointing out the same moral: that romantic fantasy and sexual attraction are poor and inadequate bases for marriage and lasting friendship. It is not, after all, that Austen is blind to the charms of beauty and wit, but she recognizes them as no more than they are. 'Beauty is skin deep' she repeatedly points out: Mr Wickham, Willoughby in *Sense and Sensibility*, and Mary Crawford in *Mansfield Park* are all presented as charming, attractive, and graceful, but their surface charms are all shown to be precisely that. But demonstrating that physical beauty is no necessary guide to moral qualities is only one side of Austen's discussion of the social construction of attractiveness: the other is that she shows that individuals, even if not blessed with outstanding good looks, can project other – equally suspect – qualities of appeal. Henry Crawford in *Mansfield Park* demonstrated this quality of subtle appeal:

48

Questioning the patriarchal order

'Her brother was not handsome; no, when they first saw him, he was absolutely plain, black and plain; but still he was the gentleman, with a pleasing address. The second meeting proved him not so very plain; he was plain, to be sure, but then he had so much countenance, and his teeth were so good, and he was so well made, that one soon forgot he was plain; and after a third interview, after dining in company with him at the parsonage, he was no longer allowed to be called so by anybody. He was, in fact, the most agreeable young man the sisters had ever known, and they were equally delighted with him.'[4]

Indeed, not only are the sisters delighted with him, they both proceed to fall in love with him. Even Fanny Price, the moral centre of Mansfield Park and the character who represents the values Austen holds most dear, becomes attracted by Henry Crawford's charm and intelligence. And the source of his appeal, as Jane Austen so perceptively suggests, is that he combines in one person both masculine and feminine qualities. The Bertram sisters and Fanny Price have all been brought up in a world in which on the whole the sexes are dichotomized in terms of activity and passivity, affectivity and non-affectivity. Sir Thomas Bertram personifies traditional patriarchal authority: absolute, unbending, and unimaginative. Lady Bertram is the passive female *par excellence*, she is passive in the physical sense of seldom leaving her sofa, and passive too in the sense of never attempting to exert any conscious control or influence over individuals and events. The 'active' male son – Tom Bertram – is a competitive young man, much exercised with his horses and his dogs. The more pensive brother, Edmund, is less physically active: unlike Tom he walks rather than rides, and occasionally joins the ladies in conversation. But Henry Crawford is at once active physically and engaging and competent in those more domestic arts of conversation and reading. In all, he appears to be a man who unites traditional masculinity with feminine concern and competence in personal relationships. In a society which separates the worlds of the sexes and the expected characteristics of men and women, Henry Crawford is a figure of great romance and fantasized longing.

Unfortunately for all concerned with him, he turns out to be morally flawed. That same ability that could make him attractive to women – the sensitivity and the quickness of wit – was also the quality, Austen suggests, that made him too liable to follow his own inclinations and pursue schemes of emotional interest and potential danger. Excessive emotionality, or excessive interest in the possibilities of human affections and relationships, is as potentially dangerous as is its absence, since it is, of course, in part the complete absence of affectivity and interest in emotional life on the part of Sir Thomas Bertram and Mr Rushworth that drives Maria Bertram into the arms of Henry Crawford. Here again we return to Jane Austen's warning against romance, but in a more complex and subtle form: she points to the danger of attempting to make good the deficiencies of sexual segregation through transcendent relationships and the appeal of qualities that are founded in need rather than principle. There can hardly be a heterosexual woman or man who does not fantasize about a Henry Crawford or a Mary Crawford: an individual who unites the most appealing qualities of both sexes. But the need for this fantasy – and the origin of the fantasy – is no guide to the validity of the character of the individual. Austen's sterling male characters (Mrs Knightley, Mr Darcy, and Captain Wentworth, for example) do not, therefore, engage in behaviour outside the conventional limits of masculinity – they do not act in plays, or read aloud in excessively dramatic ways, or amuse themselves by playing at flirtatious games. In all, they act entirely within the boundaries of a sex-segregated society and do not encourage women to indulge in romantic fantasies about them.

Nor do they meet, or court, women in romantic and essentially fantastical terms. What becomes clear from reading Austen is that she is highly suspicious of those encounters between men and women which seem to be located outside reality – where common cause is made in terms of identification with or sympathy for a particular poet, or a particular point of view that is expressed not through the direct exchange of ideas between individuals but through the mediation of a third (absent) party – a poet, novelist, or essayist. It is not, of course, that Austen does not expect her characters to exchange ideas, express opinions, and identify their tastes; on the contrary, she expects them to do all these things. But it is the nature of the exchange which she questions: the belief that a common taste for poetry, or dancing, or the representation of nature, is in any sense a viable foundation for marriage and the concerns, constraints, and responsibilities of adult social and family life. Thus throughout her novels, Austen suggests that those relationships between men and women which prove to be the most unhappy are those where the individuals meet in a fantasy world. In *Sense and Sensibility* Marianne Dashwood sees Willoughby – almost literally – as the man of her dreams because his tastes for poetry, music, and fiction coincide with hers. As her sister somewhat tersely remarks:

' "Well, Marianne," said Elinor, as soon as he had left them, "for one morning I think you have done pretty well. You have already ascertained Mr. Willoughby's opinion in almost every matter of importance. You know what he thinks of Cowper and Scott; you are certain of his estimating their beauties as he ought, and you have received every assurance of his admiring Pope no more than is proper. But how is your acquaintance to be long supported, under such extraordinary dispatch of every subject for discourse? You will soon have exhausted each favourite topic. Another meeting will suffice to explain his sentiments on picturesque beauty, and second marriages, and then you can have nothing further to ask."[5]'

Elinor is quite right to ask how the acquaintance can be supported, since it becomes rapidly clear that the relationship has no possible existence in reality: Willoughby and

Marianne have no money, and Willoughby's fantasies of riches and comfort prevent him from putting his affections for Marianne to the test. Fantastical projections of the perfect woman and the perfect man create the relationship, fantasies of the good life prevent its realization.

But perhaps the most vivid representation in all of Austen's fiction of the disjunction, indeed the difference, between fantasy and reality, is in the section of *Mansfield Park* which deals with the presentation of the play *Lover's Vows* at Mansfield Park. Bored with the usual pastimes of the country, and influenced by Tom Bertram's friend Mr Yates, the young people at Mansfield decide, in Sir Thomas's absence, to stage Kotzebue's play. Two of the central characters in the play, Baron Wildenhaim (played by Henry Crawford) and his daughter Amelia (played by Mary Crawford), make powerful cases for libertarian sexuality, and the whole of the drama is a plea for romantic love, unfettered by convention. What the production of the play provides is, however, less an opportunity for discussion of conventional morality than the frequent intimacy of Henry Crawford and Maria Bertram – cast in the role of a peasant girl seduced by Baron Wildenhaim. What has been the case in fiction is exactly what Henry and Maria would like to be the case in fact: in acting out their parts they also act out those feelings for each other which cannot be expressed in reality. For Maria Bertram (and perhaps for women) in particular, fantasy becomes overpowering; she believes herself in love with Crawford, and he with her. The bitter disillusionment when she finds that he has no intention of establishing the relationship, of giving fantasy reality, drives her into the eventually disastrous marriage with Rushworth. Only Fanny, of the young people at Mansfield, sees moral dangers in the production of the play; only she, and Jane Austen, can perceive the potential dangers of some ideological constructions of sexual desire. As Fanny realized, human beings are permeable creatures, and less than perfectly resistant to ideologies which apparently represent real need.

Questioning the patriarchal order

Austen's constant reiteration of the theme of the danger of romance and sexual fantasy is entirely in keeping with modern feminist views on the subject. Unlike previous male authors such as Henry Fielding, or later female authors, for example Charlotte and Emily Brontë, Austen takes a long and cool look at relationships founded on such socially constructed values as physical attraction and a perception of need that is closer to fantasy than to fact. And it is this distinction between real and imagined need that allows Austen to make many of her female characters into such entirely adult, and fully moral, beings. It would be easy to assume, on the basis of our modern expectations, that the ability to form mature judgements, assess character, and act well towards others is at least in some sense related to education and experience of the world. Indeed, in the twentieth century we have come to see education as the *sine qua non* of the mature adult. A long tradition in feminism has accepted and encouraged this view. From Mary Wollstonecraft to Betty Friedan and Simone de Beauvoir the argument has been made that education for women will free them from dependence and constraint. Now it is not an argument against formal education *per se* to say that Austen shows women who have lived lives of domestic seclusion nevertheless acting in ways that suggest a genuine capacity for thought and choice. So Austen does not conclude, like many feminists, that women can educate themselves out of subjectivity and subjection to patriarchal codes: she is suggesting that for women, like men, the way out of being a subject and towards at least a measure of personal autonomy is through the acceptance of and adherence to a sense of values and moral principles. Two examples of this capacity for moral choice – and morality is at the centre of Austen's concerns – are Anne Elliot in *Persuasion* and Elinor Dashwood in *Sense and Sensibility*. In both cases the heroines are assailed by values other than their own, and in both cases some of those values could be said to be derived directly from self-interested patriarchy. Anne Elliot maintains an independence of affections when her father encourages a suitable marriage partner, whilst Elinor Dashwood maintains the principle that the man she loves should honour his previous commitment to another woman. Rather than doing her best to grab her chosen partner in the marriage market, she accepts that other women besides herself have claims on him.

But the character in Austen's fiction who takes on patriarchy at its most seductive and powerful is Fanny Price in *Mansfield Park*. Fanny Price has been adopted by the Bertram family and brought up by them. Raised as a nonentity in the Bertram household she nevertheless attracts, and sustains, the affections of Henry Crawford. What began, on Henry's side, as an idle flirtation becomes a serious affair – and one in which he eventually proposes marriage. It is a match that would be, in social terms, spectacular for Fanny. From being a penniless cousin she would be transformed into the wife of a wealthy man, a man with estates and social status. But Fanny refuses Crawford. For her, Crawford is morally suspect, and she entertains a lasting affection for her cousin Edmund that Crawford has been unable to supplant. Fanny's refusal of Crawford brings down on her head the full wrath of patriarchal rationality and authority. In a very painful interview, Sir Thomas accuses Fanny of ingratitude and wilfulness:

'I had thought you peculiarly free from wilfulness of temper, self-conceit, and every tendency to that independence of spirit, which prevails so much in modern days, even in young women, and which in young women is offensive and disgusting beyond all common offence. But you have now shown me that you can be wilful and perverse, that you can and will decide for yourself, without any consideration or deference for those who have surely some right to guide you – without even asking their advice.'[6]

This speech by Sir Thomas must strike terror in modern hearts and minds, just as it did to Fanny Price in the early nineteenth century. Here is a penniless woman, who depends on the man speaking to her for everything she eats and the very roof over her head, being told that any exercise of independent will or personal choice is 'perverse', 'offensive', and 'disgusting'. Nowhere perhaps in all of Austen's fiction is male power so nakedly and unashamedly expressed as in the passage above. It is a call to arms for feminism, and suggests very precisely the kind of familial authoritarianism that thousands of women were, and still are, subject to. When Charlotte Brontë's Jane Eyre cries that however poor, however friendless, she still 'cares for herself' she is in a sense inheriting the mantle of Fanny Price by asserting in the face of Rochester's charms and her own inclinations, a moral independence and tenacity. We might, perhaps consider that Jane Eyre has an even more difficult choice than Fanny Price: after all she did deeply love Rochester, whereas Fanny Price never felt anything warmer than a sense of gratitude for Henry Crawford.

Whatever the similarities, or the differences, between the situation of Fanny Price and Jane Eyre, one thing unites them: a determination to exercise judgement and autonomy in situations where they are both under intense pressure to comply with the demands of men. Sir Thomas is not, of course, suggesting to Fanny that she should become Crawford's mistress – on the contrary, his expectations are of the most conventional and respectable kind. Nevertheless, what unites the cases is that men are attempting to get women to do what they want by the exercise of power: in the case of Sir Thomas the power is social, overlaid with emotional manipulation through guilt. In Rochester's case the power is sexual: a demand that his needs should be met and that the force of his attraction for Jane should become the basis of their relationship. Both women say no, and in doing so constitute an explicitly feminist assertion of the rights of women to self-determination. In both cases the authors show that the choice, the determination to maintain a decision, is not easy: patriarchy can be attractive – and agreeing to its demands can be a pleasant option.

Yet Jane Austen has suggested in *Mansfield Park* that

55

patriarchy has no moral justification if it is based on the law
of a father hostile to non-material values and the interests of
women. In the conclusion to *Mansfield Park* we find Sir
Thomas a shattered patriarch. Fanny is proved correct in her
judgement of Henry Crawford, Julia Bertram has eloped with
a silly young man, and Maria Bertram, now Mrs Rushworth,
has entered into an adulterous relationship with Henry
Crawford. The carefully nurtured family estates are
threatened by problems in the West Indies and by the
extravagance of Tom Bertram, the eldest son. Throughout
the invasion of Mansfield Park by the Crawfords and their
London values and habits, only Fanny has remained consistent, loyal, and unchanging in her principles. The young
woman whom Sir Thomas accused of wilfulness and per-
versity becomes acknowledged as the moral core of the
house: after her marriage to Edmund, Sir Thomas's views on
Fanny change radically:

> 'It was a match which Sir Thomas's wishes had even
> forestalled. Sick of ambitious and mercenary connections,
> prizing more and more the sterling good of principle and
> temper, and chiefly anxious to bind by the strongest
> securities all that remained to him of domestic felicity, he
> had pondered with genuine satisfaction on the more than
> possibility of the two young friends finding their mutual
> consolation in each other. . . . After settling her [Fanny] at
> Thornton Lacey with every kind attention to her comfort,
> the object of almost every day was to see her there, or to get
> her away from it.[7]'

Vindicated by the actions of others, Fanny Price has challenged patriarchy and emerged victorious – both in moral and
material terms.

Now an alternative reading of *Mansfield Park* could be
this: if Fanny Price had married Henry Crawford, then
Edmund would have married Mary Crawford, and the marriage of Maria Bertram and Mr Rushworth would have
remained intact – unsatisfactory perhaps to both parties but

nevertheless unbroken by Maria's divorce and social disgrace and exile. To many feminists, this conclusion might seem, in structural terms, to be exactly the same as the resolution contrived by Austen: the institution of heterosexual marriage is maintained, social and sexual life continues to be regulated in the same way as before, and nobody disturbs or questions the values of bourgeois marriage. It is absolutely true that in the development of her plots and characters Austen is not interested in the criticism of the institutions of bourgeois society; rather she is concerned with the values that individuals attach to these institutions and their motives for involvement in them. And here surely is a telling feminist point – not, by any means, the only feminist point of view, but one which asks important questions about the moral behaviour of men and women. Austen is asking that men and women should behave in the same ways: no toleration of the double standard of sexual morality here and little comfort for women who would like to feel that their less than impeccable behaviour can be excused by need, social pressure, or the injustices of the social world. It is not a comfortable moral world, in the sense that Austen is not a moral relativist, neither does she believe that a person's acknowledged needs and desires should condone their actions. For example, she knows full well that Maria Bertram 'needs' to escape from the overbearing paternal authority of Sir Thomas, and she does not attempt to hide from the readers Maria's misery at living under the patriarchal yoke:

'Independence was more needful than ever; the want of it at Mansfield more sensibly felt. She was less and less able to endure the restraint which her father imposed. She must escape from him and Mansfield as soon as possible, and find consolation in fortune and consequence, bustle and the world, for a wounded spirit. . . . In all the important preparations of the mind she was complete; being prepared for matrimony by a hatred of home, restraint and tranquility; by the misery of disappointed affection, and contempt of the man she was to marry.[8]

So Maria marries Rushworth as an escape from home: all
the marriages contracted in Austen's fiction for less than
worthy motives eventually become as unsatisfactory (although less disastrously and publicly so) as the Rushworths'.
The point is not therefore anti-marriage; it is an argument
against the circumstances which force individuals, men or
women, to put material and social advantage before respect
and a shared sense of values. Austen therefore mounts a
considerable case against a society which encourages in
individuals material greed and social status, and devalues, or
undervalues, the principles of care for others and genuine
concern for their welfare. In a patriarchal society it is
inevitably men rather than women who control and own
property and manipulate social status, but Austen is at pains
to show that although men may be the more active sex in
terms of the promulgation of the aims and values of a market
economy, women are just as likely to be influenced in their
actions by these values. This may not be an acceptable
message for some feminists for if the essential goodness of
women, as opposed to the essential badness of men, is a
central organizing principle of feminist analysis, then Austen
is entirely unacceptable. On the other hand, if feminism is
construed to be about the defence and articulation of values
that are non-material, that place importance on individual
happiness and the mutual support and comfort that people
can offer to one another, then Austen stands firmly within a
feminist camp, for her novels are – as much as they are
concerned with the affirmation of a socially valid moral code
– powerful statements on the importance of the domestic
world, mutuality and respect between the sexes, and the
rights of women to self-determination.

The value that Austen places on the domestic world is, as
any feminist must recognize, double-edged and somewhat
contradictory as far as modern women are concerned. To
endorse the importance of the hearth and the home, and
women's part in their maintenance, is entirely praiseworthy
– but the problem with this attitude is that it can lead to a

simple identification of women with the home and family responsibilities. As the Wages for Housework Campaign demonstrated, campaigns to improve the status of housework, and houseworkers, can backfire if they do not also attack the rigid sexual division of labour. Austen is not, of course, writing about a class which did its own housework in the literal sense; even the poorest families in her novels (the Dashwoods in *Sense and Sensibility* and the Prices in *Mansfield Park*) are able to afford some domestic assistance and we do not see any of her heroines engaged in anything more exhausting than needlework. So Austen's married couples do not argue about the division of domestic labour: the household tasks, and to a large extent the care and supervision of young children, are performed by servants.

Nevertheless, Austen does praise the competence of women at running households and emphasizes the importance that men should place on the home and domestic life. The most positive male characters in Jane Austen's fiction (Mr Knightley, Captain Wentworth, Mr Darcy, Colonel Brandon, and Edward Ferrars) all place importance on their homes, and on the maintenance of domestic life. Clearly, in the case of the wealthy men (Mr Knightley, Mr Darcy, Colonel Brandon) there is more than a sentimental attachment involved here, for what is valued is more than a small detached house. Pemberley and Donwell Abbey – the homes of Mr Darcy and Mr Knightly – are large and valuable estates, on which numerous people depend for their livelihood. Nevertheless, Mr Knightley, Mr Darcy, *et al.* are not simply concerned to extract surplus value from their estates: these constitute land and life, to be cultivated and cared for. They are not agricultural entrepreneurs, but individuals whose central concern is the maintenance of an established social life.[9] The centre of this life is the home, the place where, above all, these men are shown as delighting in passing their time. 'Domestic' is therefore a term of praise for men as far as Austen is concerned: Julia Bertram's husband, in *Mansfield Park*, is transformed into an acceptable son-in-law

59

when Sir Thomas Bertram gradually realizes that he is 'tolerably domestic'.[10] Men who regard their homes as nothing other than places in which to sleep and eat in between hunting and visits to inns and taverns (the Tom Bertrams and Mr Prices of Austen's world) are regarded as deviant and irresponsible. Home is where men as well as women belong, and it is up to men as well as women to play a part in making the home both comfortable and instructive and interesting to the young.

An example of a father who makes a home comfortable, but far from instructive, is Sir Thomas Bertram. His stress on formal values and a rigid code of manners left little place for the more important consideration of how those values might be put into practice. But Sir Thomas is not the only example of the faulty father and patriarch, Mr Bennet is another example of the man whose lack of concern for his children's moral education, indeed his complete abdication of responsibility for the care of his daughters, leads to the development of absurd follies in the case of two of them. His daughter Lydia, uneducated and unguided by anyone approaching a reasonable person, thinks only of young men, whilst her sister Mary abandons reality for pedantry and sententiousness. Mr Bennet clearly prefers his study to the world outside: given that at least part of the domestic space is occupied by Mrs Bennet, many readers find it very hard to blame him for this. Nevertheless, Jane Austen points out – with strict and absolute fairness – that the silliness of Lydia and the pomposity of Mary are not the responsibility of Mrs Bennet alone. It is an interesting and radical assertion in our culture – for we tend to assume that it is always the mother who is responsible for the behaviour of children. The 'good mother' is widely assumed to be the significant influence in a family, and it is further taken for granted that it is the responsibility of women to educate their children and supervise their moral development. So here is Jane Austen saying something that goes against this commonsense view of the patriarchy: men, she writes, are also responsible for their children, and if these turn out to be ridiculous or selfish, then parents, and not just mothers, are to blame. The idleness of Mr Bennet as far as his family is concerned is clearly spelt out to us – thus Jane Austen writes of Mr Bennet's arrangements for Lydia's marriage to Wickham:

> That it should be done with such trifling exertion on his side, too, was another very welcome surprise; for his chief wish at present, was to have as little trouble in the business as possible. When the first transports of rage which had produced his activity in seeking her were over, he naturally returned to all his former indolence. His letter was soon dispatched; for though dilatory in undertaking business, he was quick in its execution.[11]

Mr Bennet is often witty, often accurate in his judgements, but as Austen points out he is also negligent in his concern for his children's welfare.

So unlike later Victorian (also twentieth-century) moralists, Jane Austen does not lay the work and responsibility involved in the care of children and the home at the feet of women. She certainly values good housekeeping (and thus in strict justice she has to admit that however odious, Mrs Norris is an excellent housekeeper) but equally she does not assume that this skill is only to be valued by, and amongst, women. In terms of her values she is concerned that men should also respect this competence and play their part in their children's education. The role of the father as the punitive parent – the severe father and hated parent who so often appears in Dickens and other nineteenth-century fiction – is condemned before his appearance in Austen's treatment of Sir Thomas Bertram. He is, as already suggested, the Victorian paterfamilias *par excellence*; yet his deficiencies and their consequences are very clearly spelt out in *Mansfield Park*. This is not a novel which upholds patriarchal authority; on the contrary it exposes its manifest shortcomings.

The expectation that men should contribute actively to

domestic life is a major feminist demand. It is true that our understanding of the nature of this contribution is hardly the same as Jane Austen's – contemporary feminism's stress on the more equitable division of domestic labour would include those domestic tasks never named in Austen's fiction, whilst her emphasis on moral responsibility and concern is not listed in the demands of today's feminists. Nevertheless, the concerns of Jane Austen and contemporary feminism are essentially the same: that men and women should *both* construct and value domestic life, and that the sexes should jointly share the responsibilities of parenthood. Indeed, the prominence of domestic life in Austen's fiction represents an important feminist development in the history of fiction. The eighteenth-century novelists who dominated English fiction – Fielding, Richardson, and Defoe – all wrote of the public world, the open road, and the exotic place. It is true that Richardson's *Clarissa* is deeply sympathetic to women, and much concerned with the excesses of patriarchy, but the resolution of the novel does not suggest any possible negotiation between the sexes. Nor, indeed, does Richardson place much value on domestic life or apply his imagination or intelligence to the discussion of those mundane but essential concerns of domestic life – namely how a household will maintain itself, how its relationships with kin and friends will be carried on, and how children will be educated and provided for.

But Austen's eye for the importance of material factors in the construction of personal and family happiness strikes an important blow against the idea that women live in a vague, romantic space in which money does not matter. As she shows, money is crucial to women: given their limited possibilities for supporting themselves, it is essential that they consider the question of how they are going to maintain themselves and their children. To Austen, the world is not a romantic place in which men and women can form relationships that never have to be located in material reality; on the contrary, the relationships with the best chance of success

62

are those in which the contracting parties have considered with some care the circumstances in which they live. Both men and women are expected to consider this issue: Austen is not advocating the lack of responsibility of women for the material world and she is endorsing very firmly the belief that heroines *should* bother their heads about economic reality. The dream world of patriarchal romance suggests exactly the opposite: women have no material obligations in Mills and Boon romance. Such ideologies correspond exactly with the institutional practices of the state, which place economic responsibilities firmly with men. For Austen, however, the sexes have equal responsibilities – both moral and material – for the world which they, and their children, will inhabit.

Women, men, and
the state

When Jane Austen sat and composed her novels, often shielding her work from critical gaze, we should not suppose that she wrote with the interests and concerns of the bourgeois state in mind. Her intention, which is perfectly matched by her achievements, was to show how 'three or four families' in the quiet of the country conduct their daily lives and order and establish their social relationships. Yet all her novels show an understanding of the world outside the quiet of the country village; indeed, considerable sections of *Persuasion, Sense and Sensibility*, and *Mansfield Park* are set not in rural isolation but in urban centres. The world which her characters inhabit is not, therefore, as isolated or as confined as some readings of her work might suggest; on the contrary, by the standards of the late eighteenth century her characters are citizens of the world and demonstrably familiar with fashion, with the artefacts of urban culture, with developed and sophisticated manners, and with the debates of contemporary social and political life. Life in a country village was not, therefore, cut off from worldly concerns and information: Jane Austen is, after all, writing about (and in) the settled and cultivated southern counties.

So the sense of separation between town and country that is sometimes read into Austen is, perhaps, very much a twentieth-century reading. Much closer to Austen's own conception might be a model of the world as a single social construct, with the same social relationships conducted in more or less crowded and noisy places. It is not, therefore (as I have already suggested in an earlier chapter), that town life *per se* corrupts, but that the greater opportunities for corruption that exist in towns (through fashion and the conspicuous parade of wealth) can mislead or seduce the credulous or the morally inadequate. The power of towns over the morally circumspect and developed characters is non-existent: we do not need to see Mr Knightley in a town to know that his sense of himself, and his own understanding and code of values, would not be vulnerable to the temptations of a parade of power or conspicuous consumption. We know, anyway, that Mr Knightley has no objection to the process, or the results, of accumulation: his reservations are about the way in which people dispose of their surplus income. Thus even his wedding is a modest affair; as Mrs Elton incredulously observes, 'Very little white satin, very few lace veils; a most pitiful business! – Selina would stare when she heard of it.'[1]

But Mrs Elton – like Lucy Steele, Maria Bertram, Sir Walter Elliot, and numerous others in Austen's fiction – demonstrates an attitude to money and the material world that represents – to the obvious disapproval of Jane Austen – a crucial acceptance of the values of the emergent bourgeois state. Three themes therefore suggest that Austen expresses, throughout her work, a significant scepticism about the values of the market economy and the social and political relationships emerging in the early nineteenth century. The first is her understanding of the part that material factors should play in human relationships, the second is her claim for the moral equality of the sexes, and the third is her emphasis on the importance of maintaining social harmony and consensus through mutual accommodation and not through coercion. Far from being a conservative – in anything other than the superficial sense of possessing a disinclination to value change for itself – Jane Austen therefore represents that tradition in English culture which has consistently, from the seventeenth century, opposed arbitrary aristocratic and patriarchal privilege and has en-

65

dorsed and maintained values that are not derived from the market-place and the concerns and the dictates of the process of capital accumulation. It is a tradition which in Jane Austen's own day opposed the slave trade and supported the extension of the franchise and democratic access to the process of government, and which in the nineteenth and twentieth centuries opposed those results of industrial capitalism which barbarized and brutalized human existence. That the British state did emerge – at least until recently – as a set of coalitions of powerful institutions in which provision was established for the sick and vulnerable is in part a result of those values endorsed and reiterated in the quiet southern villages of Jane Austen's England: values which opposed the onslaught of the cash nexus.

The case for Austen's liberalism must, however, be made in precise terms, particularly in so far as her attitude to wealth is concerned. Her noted precision about money and income demonstrates an understanding of the processes through which social life is maintained and constructed: what she realizes, and is able to show, is that wealth can never create virtue or integrity: the rich are not necessarily the most morally defensible, nor is their behaviour any necessary guide to the most appropriate forms of conduct. In this vein, she attacks the aristocratic assumption that theirs is the prerogative of moral leadership. The aristocracy, in Jane Austen as much as in Richardson's *Clarissa*, is viewed with scepticism and detachment. But beyond what is a commonly expressed view of the aristocracy by the bourgeoisie and the *petite bourgeoisie* is a more complex set of social attitudes: Austen is not just expressing doubt about the aristocracy's ability to provide moral leadership, she is also asking questions about the nature of social hierarchy, about the proper extent of social power, and about the nature of ambition in a competitive and socially divided society. Laurence Stone has recently challenged the belief that there was an 'open' élite in Britain in the late eighteenth and early nineteenth centuries: what he is able to show is what in a

sense Jane Austen knew, that the wealthy, the significantly
rich and powerful landowners of pre-industrial England,
maintained their social position in terms of both status and
material power, through a careful balancing act between
different needs and pressures. Stone writes:

'For 340 years, the elite maintained a highly stable social
and political system, the result of a most delicate and
precarious balancing act between several sets of opposing
extremes. In their family arrangements they had had to
steer between the pursuit of too many and too few
heiresses; between producing too few and too many children; between allowing too little or too much individual
discretion in the disposal of property; between too generous expenditures which ran up debt or too miserly expenditures which created a seat too expensive to live in, or
underbuilding which led to status derogation. In their
behaviour towards other classes they had had to steer
between too generous paternalism towards tenants which
would erode revenues, and too ruthless profiteering which
would undermine deference; between too ready acceptance
of the new rich which would dilute numbers and values,
and too rigid rejection which would stimulate class anta-
gonism. In their political capacities they had had to
manoeuvre between too gross an exploitation of public
offices which would engender public opprobrium and
governmental inefficiency, and too ready a welcome to
reform which would substitute merit for influence and thus
might erode one basis of their family fortunes; between the
cherished ideals of popular sovereignty and the rule of law,
and a practical arrangement which preserved power in
elite hands. It was a difficult balancing act, which was
fairly astutely managed throughout the sixteenth, seventeenth, eighteenth and even the early and mid-nineteenth
centuries.
As a result, in most respects, the relative financial
resources, background, education, and way of life of a

member of the landed elite in 1880 were not all that different from what they had been in 1680.'

(Stone and Stone 1984: 422)

But the 'difficult balancing act' of which Stone writes was not, of course, to be achieved by magic: it was achieved through precisely the careful calculation of the social world that Jane Austen articulated and endorsed in her novels. If we take any of those vital ingredients of social stability which are mentioned by Stone we find them in Austen. For example, ruthless profiteering is ruled out by the two large landowners of Austen's fiction: Mr Knightley and Mr Darcy. The rejection of the new rich and the newly socially significant by the aristocracy is condemned in *Persuasion* in Austen's critical discussion of Sir Walter Elliot's behaviour towards Admiral and Mrs Croft and Captain Wentworth. In the same novel, Lady Russell stands condemned for having too great an enthusiasm for rank rather than talent and enterprise. In every novel, order and consensus are praised; by contrast, individual attempts to gain social ascendancy and privilege through suspect means are exposed and criticized.

This gives the individual in Austen's novels, and indeed in any market economy, be it fictitious or otherwise, a difficult path to tread. Contemporary and historical evidence suggests that at least two-thirds of the population of any capitalist society are born into the world (and leave it) with nothing, or in any case with considerably less than some of the more fortunate characters in Austen's fiction. However, the structural problem for many individuals in the real world is exactly the same as that which confronts Fanny and William Price and the Dashwood sisters: born with little or nothing that will guarantee social and material support, how are individuals to survive if not by simple, straightforward self-interest and selfish self-absorption? The social system, as it was and still is, will provide only a minimal level of support;

anything approaching a 'good' life must be achieved by
individual effort. So individuals are placed, in the context of
capitalist social relations, in a situation of constant and
complex moral contradiction. They are faced, on the one
hand, with the need to maintain themselves, on the other,
with a moral code, endorsed by the Christian church, that
suggests that to seek excessive wealth is suspect, and to love
money, or the process of accumulation, is even more so. It is
clear from the history of England since the seventeenth
century that numerous rich people took their chance on
passing through the eye of a needle and the English countryside is littered with the evidence of highly successful
exercises in appropriation. Nevertheless, while the great
estates and houses of Marlborough, Chatsworth, Blenheim,
et al., exist as testaments to the ability of the English
aristocracy to create and amass wealth, the charitable
organizations that flourished from the eighteenth century
onwards suggest that the ethic of personal self-
agrandizement was not the only impetus behind the behaviour of the aristocracy and the bourgeoisie. Social
consciences, however limited and however inadequate, were
none the less aware of the miseries of industrialization and
agricultural depression, and did mitigate some of the excesses of an economic system which did not contain within
itself any checks, except those of financial success or failure,
on the process of the accumulation of profit.

Individual decisions about how to live within capitalism
could, then, make a significant difference to the lives of other
people living within that same social formation. We do not,
therefore, find in Jane Austen the voice of an author who is
advocating individual responsibility in the sense that it has
now come to be construed by some conservatives: an ethic
which allows individuals to act in their best interests
regardless of the cost to others. Jane Austen's message is
more complex: she fully accepts that individuals have a
responsibility for themselves, yet at the same time she
recognizes the socially and individually disruptive possibi-

lities of behaviour that is only organized around personal enrichment and survival. Individuals, she realizes, cannot survive without one another, and although she is far from supposing that we actually have to love one another or die (an idea which she would perhaps have regarded as fanciful in the extreme) she is pointing out to her readers that whatever the temptations of individualism, the rewards are often empty, illusory, and lonely. Greed for money and social position, the desire for sexual confirmation and endorsement: all these lusts are shown by Austen to be not merely wrong, but unsatisfying in their rewards.

What this must suggest is that, first, Austen regards the profit motive with great suspicion and that, second, she views with equal caution the supposed dictates of need and desire. Both impulses are, she points out to her readers, to be approached with great caution, since they are most easily and often most fully, socially constructed. Over a hundred years before Freud she recognized that civilization lies not in the immediate gratification of human impulses, but in their sublimation and organization. Like Freud she recognized that actual repression holds dangers: the society created at *Mansfield Park* by the repressive authority of Sir Thomas Bertram is precisely the kind of world in which fanciful, exaggerated, and in the event undisciplined, desires and fantasies flourish. Two adolescent girls, expected to be content with formal society and inadequate, and unknown, adult company, became the prey of the first personable man whom they meet. The sheltered – in the moral and the personal sense – Bertram sisters fall for Henry Crawford with as much enthusiasm as Jane Eyre for Rochester, or Catherine Earnshaw for Heathcliff: in all cases the isolation of women provides a perfect breeding ground for the development of fantasies about the powers of men to provide an explanation, and indeed a justification, for existence.

In *Mansfield Park* Jane Austen presents to us the most perfect, developed, metaphor about the nature of social isolation, sexual repression, and social constraint. On a day

trip to Mr Rushworth's country house, Mary and Henry
Crawford, Julia and Maria Bertram, Edmund Bertram,
Fanny Price, and Mr Rushworth all take an afternoon walk
in the grounds of the estate. The day is hot, and in order to
seek some shade, the party turn into a wood. Or, as Mary
Crawford puts it:

> 'This is insufferably hot. . . . Shall any of us object to being
> comfortable? Here is a nice little wood, if one can but get into
> it. What happiness if the door should not be locked! – but of
> course it is, for in these great places, the gardeners are the
> only people who can go where they like.'[2]

The 'comfort' to which Mary Crawford alludes is both the
literal comfort of shade on a hot day and the metaphorical
comfort of a natural world, away from the harsh glare and
reality of the wealth of Sotherton. Amongst the trees and the
cool green light of the wood it is possible for the party to
speak more easily and more naturally – and they do, with
revealing results. Thus away from the formal world of polite
manners Mary Crawford makes clear her contempt for the
priesthood and exposes that social cynicism which is eventually to alienate her from Edmund Bertram for ever. Maria
Bertram demonstrates with absolute clarity her contempt for
Mr Rushworth, and in sending him on a fool's errand shows
that she is prepared to use him both particularly and
generally in the fulfilment of her own needs. Exposure to
nature does not therefore reveal anything but the negative
side of Maria Bertram and Henry and Mary Crawford. The
positive characters – Edmund, Fanny, and even, it has to be
allowed, Mr Rushworth – are not creatures whose behaviour
is a construct for the formal world: their behaviour is
consistent and integrated. Mr Rushworth remains stupid
wherever he is, but the sincerity of his intentions, and his
desire to please, are sufficiently genuine for him to rush
around on a hot day solely for the convenience of others.
But within the seclusion of the quiet wood at Sotherton
more is revealed than the opinions of Mary Crawford on the

71

church or Maria Bertram on her fiancé – opinions which are largely known to us already. What we learn is less about specific views than the intensity of feeling between some of the characters; needs are thus revealed which never emerge in any other context. We know, therefore, after this episode, that Maria Bertram longs to escape from her father's home and that she entertains much deeper feelings for Henry Crawford than had previously been suggested. In an exchange rich in metaphor Henry Crawford and Maria reveal much about themselves and their feelings. Henry remarks to Maria that, 'Your prospects, however, are too fair to justify want of spirits. You have a very smiling scene before you.' She replies:

> ' "Do you mean literally or figuratively? Literally, I conclude. Yes, certainly, the sun shines and the park looks very cheerful. But unluckily that iron gate, that ha-ha, give me a feeling of restraint and hardship. I cannot get out, as the starling said." As she spoke, and it was with expression, she walked to the gate; he followed her. "Mr. Rushworth is so long fetching this key." "And for the world you would not get out without the key and without Mr. Rushworth's authority and protection, or I think you might with little difficulty pass round the edge of the gate, here, with my assistance; I think it might be done, if you really wished to be more at large, and could allow yourself to think it not prohibited."
>
> "Prohibited! nonsense! I certainly can get out that way, and I will." '[3]

What Maria Bertram then proceeds to do, in the gardens of Sotherton, is an anticipation of what she attempts to do in the conclusion to the novel: to cross a dangerous barrier (in this case a gate with iron spikes, in the latter instance, involvement in an adulterous affair) with no injury to herself. Yet what she manages at Sotherton she cannot manage in real life: the iron gate proves easier to cross than conventional boundaries to legitimate sexuality.

But what the conversation also contains is a veiled reference to the constraints that Maria perceives in her coming marriage. She does not accept Crawford's depiction of her prospects in either a literal or a figurative sense; indeed, she explicitly rejects the figurative possibilities of the scene, and agrees only to the material advantages of her marriage to Mr Rushworth. Her only chance of escape from this prospect is with Henry Crawford's assistance: with his collusion, he suggests, she could both have her cake and eat it. If only she could show him that she would take a chance, if only she would suggest that she would be prepared to compromise herself, then they might both pass into those forbidden places that morality and convention forbid them to enter. Maria seizes the opportunity to make her position clear: she is prepared to compromise, she is prepared to place her desire to be with Henry Crawford above all other considerations. So she passes a pleasant hour or so alone with Henry Crawford; again, the events of the day's outing to Sotherton anticipate the remainder of the novel, for the costs of the brief tête-à-tête prove to be considerable, and the satisfactions of intimacy with Henry Crawford carry the cost, in this case, of irritating the rest of the party, whilst her later adultery forces her into social exile for ever.

In the course of the day's outing to Sotherton, therefore, we have learnt a good deal both about the individual characters in *Mansfield Park* and about Jane Austen's perception of the nature of constraint. She does not endorse the view that to release people from society and convention is to allow them to flourish more fully. We are not, therefore, presented with that romantic view of human nature which sees it in its natural state as nothing except positive and generous. On the contrary, human desires – released from the constraints of social life – are too often like those of Mary Crawford and Maria Bertram: ill-informed, prejudiced, selfish, and greedy. But in the course of the walk in the gardens at Sotherton Jane Austen also suggests to us two other particularly important possibilities about human attempts to organize, structure, and – in some cases – inhibit human action. The first point that she makes is that stern restraint – the iron gate with spikes on its top, which is, in itself, a very vivid representation of prison gates in eighteenth- and nineteenth-century England – is of absolutely no effect when it comes to preventing vice or crime. There is always a key to any gate, and if no one can find or is allowed it, then someone will find a way round or over. But the second, more subtle, point that she makes is that restraints are constructs of particular situations: the gate is a very important barrier to Maria Bertram and Henry Crawford because morally they should not pass through it. However stupid Mr Rushworth and however charming Henry Crawford, it is fundamentally unacceptable from a moral point of view for Maria Bertram to use the former as a means of deceit with the latter. Yet the gate matters little to Julia Bertram or Mary Crawford and Edmund Bertram; the former vaults easily over it, the latter pair merely avoid it. Julia, therefore, has no need to see the gate as a barrier, since her behaviour is not called into question by it; Mary and Edmund are too aware of social niceties to confront them directly.

Thus constraints and formal social rules are shown to be inadequate as means of regulating behaviour. Secondly, restraint is shown to create the desire for freedom: individuals brought up in severe moral worlds, like that of Sir Thomas Bertram, will regard morality as an empty, rigid code which is essentially about prohibition, not as a self-imposed discipline or enlightening order. The social force of those codes dear to the heart of the unreconstituted Sir Thomas Bertram is thus only limited: they appear to impose order on society, but in fact do little except create deviance by the imposition of closed categories on often ambiguous patterns of human behaviour. Sir Thomas appears at precisely the point in English history when the British state was beginning to exercise an anxious control on morality and personal behaviour: the New Poor Law of 1834 and the Marriages Act of 1836 both suggest that the state (as well as both the

Established and Non-Conformist Churches) had decided, first, that a stable two-parent family was the ideal norm of family life and, second, that the state of marriage as a formal union between two people of the opposite sex must be given priority over other, less formalized, arrangements.[4] In the latter part of the nineteenth century, the state launched two comprehensive attempts at regulating sexual behaviour: the Contagious Diseases Act of 1867 (repealed in the 1880s) was but one, although perhaps the most notorious, example of exercises in controlling personal life.

Now whilst Sir Thomas Bertram can be identified as a representative of all those forces in nineteenth-century England which were repressive and rigid, we cannot identify Jane Austen with all that is liberal and free-thinking. So the argument here is not that Austen represents a tradition of liberal thinking about the organization of the family and sexuality: she is clearly not 'for' sexual unions between men and women that are not sanctioned by marriage, nor does she ever abandon her belief that marriage entails sexual fidelity for both partners. But she is liberal in two very important senses: she does not idealize the family, or make it into a legitimate locus of unquestioned patriarchal authority; nor does she sanction marriage as the only form of social life that is acceptable for human beings. Her understanding of marriage implies the mutual acceptance by both partners of a code of behaviour, but does not either prioritize married life as a more holy and socially viable state than all others; nor does she represent, in any of her novels, family life as anything except a process of constant negotiation between the partners which is often beset with difficulties and unsatisfactory arrangements. Those domestic 'interiors' so beloved of Victorian novelists and artists – the red plush, the warm fire, the gentle wife, and the acquiescent children – do not exist in Jane Austen. Instead, we are plunged into the cold elegance of Mansfield Park, the divided home of the Bennets, the squalor of Mr and Mrs Price's accommodation in Portsmouth, the noisy, child-centred households of

Charles and Mary Musgrove and Mr and Mrs Musgrove in *Persuasion*, and the calculating vapidity of Mr and Mrs John Dashwood's domestic life. In contrast to those cosy hearths portrayed by George Eliot and Charles Dickens, Jane Austen's domestic interiors suggest a critical, realistic eye, an eye which resists the ideological temptation of presenting the family as a 'haven in a heartless world'.

Thus Jane Austen, in her presentation of family life, is no idealist, and is, indeed, entirely resistant to irrational presentations of the family. She resists, moreover, any attempt to define the family as a unit which can only be maintained by (male) authority and (female) subservience: authoritarian fathers and passive mothers ruin the family and the young, she argues, just as surely as male lack of interest in the family can create over-demanding pressures for women as wives and mothers. Again we find Austen advocating balance and consensus in human relationships: in a defiant challenge to individualistic perceptions of human beings and human relations she does not find strength in human existence through individual self-definition and self-interest. On the contrary, the strongest human beings in her fiction are those who are best able to live harmoniously with others, and the value of living harmoniously, and without exaggerated individualism, is a lesson which several of her heroes and heroines have to learn. In an ethic counter to that of the self-definition and self-assertion encouraged by the ideology of the market economy, Jane Austen suggests that the ability to temper individual needs, and allow other individuals their rights of self-determination, is perhaps the most positive skill that individuals can bring to social existence.

But, as she also shows, the skill of living as a social being is one that both has to be learned and is scarcely encouraged by the economic relations of the society in which her characters live. A 'natural' mode of behaviour for individuals in late eighteenth-century and early nineteenth-century England would not be the quiet, disciplined morality of Fanny Price, but the self-important, acquisitive mode of behaviour of Mrs Elton in *Emma*, Mr Elliot in *Persuasion*, and the Steele sisters in *Sense and Sensibility*. These are, in an important sense, the characters who are formed by the values and the socialization most generally available for people living in a market economy. It is not in the interests of people living under capitalist social relations to act like Fanny Price or Elinor Dashwood: they are at odds with the dominant values of the society as surely as Mrs Elton and Lucy Steele are at one with them. Indeed, in these women, and in Maria Bertram and Mrs John Dashwood, we see the ethic of capitalism given flesh and blood, an ethic which places all social and personal relationships, and all values and sentiments, second to the demands of material enrichment. The expansiveness of capitalism in the early nineteenth century gives to these characters part of their extraordinary vitality and energy – the materially preoccupied in Jane Austen have none of the self-doubts, the indolence, or the lack of judgement of later bourgeois characters in fiction. For example, members of the Buddenbrook family in Thomas Mann's great saga of the decline of the German bourgeoisie exhibit a profound loss of interest, and indeed nerve, in the process of capital accumulation that entirely separates them from the John Dashwoods and the Steele sisters. By the early twentieth century, however, the consequences of living for accumulation had become clear to perceptive observers of the social world: the personal unhappiness and the loss of integrity occasioned by choices dictated entirely by financial self-interest had created an indifference to, and profound suspicion of, the needs and constraints of the material world.

This alienation could, perhaps, be explained by that loss of balance and compromise in human relationships in advanced industrial capitalism that Jane Austen portrays as so dangerous. When Toni Buddenbrook is forced by the financial interests of her family to marry Herr Grünlich she is sacrificed to a set of interests which leave no place for personal choice or for the establishment and development of a relationship between two human beings that might have the strength to withstand material misfortune. As it is, of course, the complete lack of mutual concern and respect between husband and wife means that as soon as material circumstances change from fortunate to deprived, the marriage collapses as there is, literally and metaphorically, nothing to hold the husband and wife together. And so capitalism can be seen, in this instance, to create the very instability in personal relationships that its ideology condemns: whilst the dominant ideology of capitalism on the subject of personal relationships states that husbands and wives, and parents and children, should owe their first loyalties to each other, and stay together whatever the circumstances, the very facts of material life are such that for many people it is impossible to live by these rules.

So what emerges in the nineteenth century is a situation in which *the state has to enforce what capitalism destroys*: as the informal fabric of responsibility and mutuality is destroyed by the material excesses and hardships of industrial capitalism, so the central organization of civil society has to establish, and enforce, codes of behaviour to replace the associations and the values that are threatened by the demands of the capitalist market. Many people, of course, have remained immune, in their personal relationships, to the constraints of the material world, but the point is rather that the development of capitalism since the end of the eighteenth century has been steadily pervasive in its relevance. Material self-interest always existed as a motive for human behaviour – greed is no invention of capitalism. But what is unique to capitalism is the nature of the opportunities for accumulation that it offers: these opportunities had been recognized by the end of the eighteenth century and were increasingly part of the world which Jane Austen knew. In the unfinished fragment of *Sandition* she introduced, as a major theme, the development of the countryside for profit, and although we never see the realization of the novel it is apparent from what exists that Jane Austen is as able as

Women, men, and the state

Thomas Mann to show characters whose very being has been taken over by the values of the market-place. These are characters who do not even, like the Miss Steeles, feel the need to blush at, or attempt to rationalize, their behaviour: a crucial point has been crossed, at which material self-interest and a ruthless spirit of accumulation are no longer problematic. There are, in fact, no longer any contradictions between the values of the market and the values of social and personal life – they are the same.

It is a feature of Jane Austen's genius that she was able to recognize and express the demands of the material world. Moreover, in her discussion of material questions and their implications, she took neither the conservative position of denying the importance of material life and retreating into romantic indifference to its maintenance nor the equally, although more obviously, conservative position of defending the importance of material questions above all others. What she tells us about material life is as relevant in the 1980s as it was in the early nineteenth century: that it is the equal responsibility of both sexes, but has to be firmly located within a set of values and principles that are not derived from the motive of property accumulation. Women are not allowed to escape from their duty to consider questions of economic life: in reality of course few women ever had this opportunity, but the ideology of Victorian Britain and romantic fiction was such as to suggest that it was the duty only of men to consider the material realities of the world.

This ideology – that the proper relationship of women to the material world is that they are provided for by men – was, however, part of the numerous attempts in the nineteenth century to remove or bar women from the most economically rewarding sections of the burgeoning Victorian economy. Many Victorian campaigns on industry and the proper place of women legitimately attempted to prevent women, and particularly women with young children, from entering the rigours and horrors of the Victorian factory and mine; but side by side with these genuinely philanthropic impulses, there also existed prejudices about the 'right' of men to better paid work. That these two views could exist in the same person or group makes it all the more confusing for students of sexual divisions and antagonisms – at best we can say that men's campaigns for a 'family wage' and restrictive practices arose from mixed motives.[5] Whatever the case, the accompanying ideology, as pervasive for the working class as for the middle class, contributed towards the development of a romantic view of women's relationship to material issues: these issues were the proper preserve of men. Thus as the social relations of production of capitalism systematically excluded women (and hence left them, in a society dominated by wage labour, with few means of provision), so the state and civil society had to develop an ideology and, eventually, laws, which attempted to impose on men the responsibility for the material provision of women and children. It is not so much, however, that women were not provided for by men – to a certain extent that had always been the case. The novel development in the nineteenth century was the systematic loss by women of their place in the household economy – leaving them dependent on the wage labour of husband or father.

Jane Austen's concerns were clearly not those of Victorian working-class women deprived of a means of supporting themselves But where she does make common cause – and radical common cause — with those women, is in her perception of the instability of material life, and the need to develop a morality between the sexes, and between individuals generally, that is not one of simple self-interest and the ordering of social relations through the mechanisms of the economic market. The challenge which her work represents is not, therefore, that of conservatism, but of radicalism: a challenge to a way of life increasingly ruled by material motives and a desire for material accumulation.

Conclusion

In pointing out and defining the inadequacies of living life according to the demands of the market economy, Jane Austen sets a moral agenda for social life and civil society. At the top of that agenda she places the question of how consensus is to be achieved in a world in which the weak can easily be trampled by the greed and strength of the rich and powerful, whose concerns are frequently legitimated as the common sense of the age. The aggressive conservatism of contemporary monetarism epitomizes precisely that ruthless self-interest which Jane Austen so deeply dislikes: a self-interest which asserts as *natural* the desire to compete (both economically and socially) and the wish of human beings to act in all things as single, isolated individuals. The 'naturalistic' fallacy of the competitive spirit has been echoed time and again in the nineteenth and twentieth centuries; ideologies of educational practice, business behaviour, and personal worth have been elaborated to develop, or demonstrate, the assumed need of human beings to compete with one another. The two beliefs – the belief in the natural instinct to compete and the belief in the natural desire of human beings to act in isolation – were regarded by Jane Austen as both dangerous and socially disruptive. People who acted in ways that sought their own profit rather than that of their neighbours, and were prepared to follow their own 'natural' inclinations and instincts whatever the cost, were shown, in her novels, to be the cause of misery to themselves and others.

Jane Austen and the State

But more than wishing to contain behaviour, Jane Austen also sought to show that individually selfish behaviour – albeit derived from integration into the values of material self-interest – creates not only individual misery but also forms of repression that distort and undermine the behaviour of others. Iron bars and locked gates can make a prison, but they cannot prevent crime or anti-social behaviour. The savage excesses of the Victorian penal system, and the harshness of Victorian institutional morality, thus find no echo in Austen: she exiles the adulterous Maria, leaves Willoughby to a life of domestic disharmony, and otherwise disposes of the selfish and nasty to live out the lives they have created for themselves. But she does not punish in the way that the Victorians were capable of punishing. Witness this incident, described by a co-worker of Elizabeth Fry:

> 'on my left hand, sat Laurence, alias Woodman, surrounded by her four children, and only waiting the birth of another, which she hourly expects, to pay the forfeit of her life. . . . I (later) found poor Woodman lying-in, in the common ward, where she had been suddenly taken ill; herself and little girl were each doing very well. What can be said of such sights as these.'[1]

It is, indeed, impossible to say a great deal about a social system which hangs mothers of five children for minor theft. But this incident, which cannot be supposed to have been the only case of its kind in Victorian England, illustrates precisely the kind of harsh punishment (which cannot be described as anything approaching justice) that Austen's conception of morality and social organization could not contain. Contemporaries of Elizabeth Fry observed that although she was a most charitable and tireless worker for the good of female prisoners, she could not emancipate herself from the belief in the right, indeed the legitimacy, of punishment by the state. It is a view that endorses the conception of a need for contrived punishment, and its implementation by institutional power.

Conclusion

Jane Austen's conception of punishment, indeed of sin and crime, is at once both more radical and more liberal than this. Herself well acquainted with the reality of the horrors of the prison system in early nineteenth-century England (an uncle's wife was imprisoned, although subsequently acquitted, following an accusation of theft), Jane Austen recognized both the brutality of punishments suffered by those accused of even the most minor theft, and the social causes of deviant behaviour. It is this which marks her from many other writers – both contemporary and subsequent – and it is this which provides justification for her being described as radical: she looks beyond the actual offence or action, and attempts to locate the cause. She does not, therefore, like true conservatives, accept the world as given, or actual human behaviour as the sum total of human possibility. It is not, she argues, 'human' nature to cheat, deceive, and compete, any more than it is 'human' nature to be honest and unselfish in personal relationships. Human beings are not, in this view, people who must do as best as they can according to the dictates of an economic market, they are people who must make choices about their actions according to principles which have little, if anything, to do with the dictates of the market economy or economic self-interest. She would not, therefore, argue that the poor should steal because they have no other way of providing for themselves: on the contrary, she is at pains to show that if people are poor this is more often than not in part because of the actions – the false choices – of others. Poverty, she recognizes, is constructed: Mrs Smith is poor because Mr Elliot cheated her; Fanny Price is poor because her father is indolent and incompetent.

But Jane Austen's chief concern is less with the construction of material poverty than with the construction of moral poverty. She realizes that attempts to repress 'immorality' are doomed to failure: the case of Sir Thomas Bertram runs parallel to many of the institutional practices of the Victorian state, which attempted to stamp out vice by repression. Austen realized that what the Victorians were to describe as 'vice' was impossible to prohibit by institutional constraints, people could only be 'good' – in the sense of thoughtful of the implications of their behaviour for others – if they both recognized their own needs and the rights of others to theirs. It is a moral code which allows for no naturalistic justifications: nobody has a 'right' to fulfil their needs, equally no one has a right to thwart or punish according to their own fears of change and the rights of others. Sir Thomas's desire to contain and control his own world thus cause his desire to repress; without that impulse, the fatal repression of his children might never have occurred.

So Austen recognizes a dialectic in human relations which makes her a complex and a far from didactic novelist. She does not wish to show the justice of a single case, or a single cause, but is at pains to reveal that human beings, men and women, construct their fates and have in their power the ability to mould their desires and temper their ambitions in ways which can produce relationships of lasting value. In this understanding of the world there is no place for moral abdication. Men cannot claim that the home is no responsibility of theirs, any more than women can claim that they are seduced or 'led astray' by men. Speaking to Elinor Dashwood of his behaviour to Colonel Brandon's ward, Willoughby argues that:

'I acknowledge that her situation and her character ought to have been respected by me. I do not mean to justify myself, but at the same time cannot leave you to suppose that I have nothing to urge – that because she was injured she was irreproachable, and because *I* was a libertine, *she* must be a saint.'[2]

A crucial defence, for it reveals Jane Austen's perception of sexual behaviour as a construct in which women are far from the passive victims of male desire. Mrs Gaskell, in writing of illegitimacy in *Ruth*, cannot bring herself to anything like the same conclusion: for her, as for many Victorian feminists and social reformers, the protection of women, and the amelioration of their situation, was only to be achieved through the definition of men as aggressors and predators. The causes for this position are not difficult to identify: given the massive harshness and brutality of Victorian institutional practices on subjects such as illegitimacy and prostitution, it is easier to argue a black and white case of female virtue and vice than a case in which the sexes may well have, if not an equal, then at least a shared responsibility for their mutual fate. Admitting the sexual desire of women – allowing the desires for sexual excitement so transparently represented by Maria Bertram – would ruin a case which rests upon the exposition of the unjust treatment of innocents.

But Jane Austen allows herself to portray sexual desire in women, and the ways in which women can make both nonsense, and sense, of men. The sensible, balanced Lady Elliot can, therefore, almost make Sir Walter appear as a reasonable man, just as the unthinking and vulgar Mrs Elton transforms her husband from a rather dull young man into a dull *and* ridiculous young man. Not, as Jane Austen shows, that his outward behaviour changes all that much: what changes is that we realize that a man who can be addressed as 'caro sposo', and choose a wife who manages to deny that her sister is a lady, is capable of being more than merely boring; he is also capable of profound lapses of judgement. Human beings are not, therefore, what they are born: they are creatures who have at their command the power to make, or break, their fates. And here, too, we find Jane Austen posing for us one of those crucial questions for students of social and human relations: how is it that individuals, born into apparently identical circumstances, can differ so much? How is it, therefore, that Elizabeth Bennet can be so lively and intelligent, when at least one of her sisters is so dull and silly? The circumstances, answers Jane Austen, are only superficially the same: look a little more closely at the Price household, or that of the Bennets, or the various worlds of the

Ward sisters, and slight, yet significant, differences between
the treatment of individuals appear, which can critically
develop existing differences of temperament. For example,
Elizabeth Bennet is her father's favourite, and so wits that
are already quick are sharpened and developed by contact
that is denied to her sisters. Again, amongst the Ward sisters
(Lady Bertram, Mrs Norris, and Mrs Price) Jane Austen
indicates the temperamental similarities between Lady Bertram and Mrs Price and then points out how their tendency
to indolence is acceptable, even appropriate, in a rich
woman, and completely unacceptable in a woman with a
wasteful and idle husband. Over and over, Jane Austen shows
us that individual differences in ability and temperament are
developed and articulated by circumstances and choice: we
are not just what we are born, we are also what the world
makes of us, and what we make of ourselves.

So in Jane Austen's worlds there are no 'born' criminals,
no 'born' libertines – none of those people whom Victorian
criminologists, doctors, and anthropologists tried so hard to
locate in their researches on criminals, foreigners, and the
lower orders in general. Nor is vice, or virtue, an attribute of
one sex: all human beings have the capacity to act well or
badly, and there are no constraints of gender on the amount
of suffering that individuals of both sexes can cause to others.
It is a view of individual human beings which allowed, long
before Marx and Freud, that people construct the world, and
yet construct it in ways that are often dangerous or limited,
made so by unmet needs, by the deep psychic horror of the
secret, by silence, and by a constant pattern of denial. 'I can
listen no longer in silence', writes Captain Wentworth to
Anne Elliot, and in doing so he breaks through convention
and practice and addresses, directly, the woman he still loves.
It is – in Jane Austen's fiction – an act of unparalleled
emotional self-assertion, a suggestion that the author had, by
the end of her life, come to see the dangers, as well as the
values, of constant emotional self-restraint.

Manufactured conventions, so ruthlessly exposed as inef-

Conclusion

fectual, indeed positively harmful, in *Mansfield Park*, are thus given the final blow in *Persuasion*. The positive side to convention – the caution that might have prevented Marianne's involvement with Willoughby or Lydia Bennet's with Wickham – are countered, in *Mansfield Park* and *Persuasion*, by its negative aspects. Rules, Jane Austen points out, can sometimes be made to be broken, and they are, in any circumstances, merely guides to behaviour. The state and civil society can legislate and establish ideologies of appropriate behaviour, but cannot, simply through the establishment of its monolithic and bureaucratic power, adequately ensure harmonious moral relationships between its citizens. Human beings, in the context of a social formation which moulds their behaviour towards the prioritization of material advantage, cannot be made good by the strictures of the state: it is only through the constant reiteration and identification of the values of mutuality, co-operation, and honesty that a society worth living in can continue.

Notes

INTRODUCTION

1 *Persuasion*, p. 237
2 At the same time as Jane Austen was writing, people outside the scope of her novels were organizing themselves in institutions of mutual assistance to combat the worst excesses of early industrial capitalism. The proletarian community, later to be documented by E.P. Thompson (1963, 1974) and others, was being established.

CHAPTER 1

1 *Emma*, p. 330.

CHAPTER 2

1 A powerful corrective to this view is given in Moers (1974) pp. 200–215.
2 *Sense and Sensibility*, p. 46.
3 The system of entailment and transfer of property in the eighteenth century has been outlined by Habakkuk (1950).
4 *Pride and Prejudice*, p. 271.
5 *Mansfield Park*, p. 434.
6 *Mansfield Park*, p. 239.
7 *Northanger Abbey*, p. 15.
8 *Sense and Sensibility*, p. 122.

CHAPTER 3

1 *Northanger Abbey*, pp. 11–12.
2 *Northanger Abbey*, p. 14.
3 *Pride and Prejudice*, p. 331.
4 *Mansfield Park*, p. 77.
5 *Sense and Sensibility*, p. 79.
6 *Mansfield Park*, p. 318.
7 *Mansfield Park*, p. 456.
8 *Mansfield Park*, p. 216.

Notes

9 The value that Jane Austen places on the careful management of estates is discussed in Duckworth (1971).
10 *Mansfield Park*, p. 447.
11 *Pride and Prejudice*, p. 323.

CHAPTER 4

1 *Emma*, p. 427.
2 *Mansfield Park*, p. 119.
3 *Mansfield Park*, pp. 126–27.
4 I do not wish to suggest here that the British state decided, out of the blue, to regulate the morality of family and social life. The Established Church had long attempted to maintain moral sanctions about personal behaviour, and the Methodist revival was centrally concerned with a more active regulation of individual behaviour. See, for a discussion of these issues, Gillis (1985: 109–34).
5 For significant contributions to this debate see Humphries (1981) and Barrett and McIntosh (1980).

CONCLUSION

1 In *Memoir of the Life of Elizabeth Fry, with Extracts from her Journal and Letters, Edited by Her Two Daughters* (1847), quoted in Murray (1984: 288).
2 *Sense and Sensibility*, p. 316.

List of works
consulted or cited in the text

THE WORKS OF JANE AUSTEN

Sense and Sensibility. Harmondsworth: Penguin, 1969.
Pride and Prejudice. Harmondsworth: Penguin, 1972.
Mansfield Park. Harmondsworth: Penguin, 1966.
Emma. London: J.M. Dent, 1961.
Northanger Abbey. New York: New American Library, 1965.
Persuasion. Harmondsworth: Penguin, 1965.
Lady Susan/The Watsons. Harmondsworth: Penguin, 1974.
Sanditon.
Jane Austen's Letters, collected and edited by R.W. Chapman. Oxford: Oxford University Press, 1979.

OTHER WORKS

Barrett, Michele and McIntosh, Mary (1980) The Family Wage: Some Problems for Socialists and Feminists. *Capital and Class* 11: 51–72.
Benjamin, Walter (1973) *Charles Baudelaire: a Lyric Poet in the Era of High Capitalism*. London: New Left Books.
Bradbrook, Frank (1966) *Jane Austen and her Predecessors*. Cambridge: Cambridge University Press.
Brontë, Charlotte *Jane Eyre*.
Brontë, Emily *Wuthering Heights*.
Butler, Marilyn (1975) *Jane Austen and the War of Ideas*. Oxford: Oxford University Press.
Cowie, C. and Lees, S. (1981) Slags or Drags? *Feminist Review* 9: 17–31.
Duckworth, Alistair (1971) *The Improvement of the Estate*. Baltimore: Johns Hopkins University Press.
Eagleton, Terry (1982) *The Rape of Clarissa*. Oxford: Blackwell.
Gaskell, Mrs *Ruth*.

List of works consulted or cited in the text

Gillis, John (1985) *For Better or for Worse, British Marriages 1600 to the Present*. Oxford: Oxford University Press.

Habakkuk, H.J. (1950) Marriage Settlements in the Eighteenth Century. *Transactions of the Royal Historical Society* XXXII: 15–30.

Halperin, John (1984) The Life of Jane Austen. Brighton: The Harvester Press.

Harding, D.W. (1963) Regulated Hatred: An Aspect of the Work of Jane Austen. In Ian Watt (ed.) *Jane Austen, a Collection of Critical Essays*. Englewood Cliffs, N.J.: Prentice Hall pp. 166–79.

Hill, Christopher (1968) Clarissa Harlowe and her Times. In *Puritanism and Revolution*. London: Panther pp. 351–76.

Hudson, Barbara (1984) Femininity and Adolescence. In Angela McRobbie and Mica Nava (eds) *Gender and Generation*. London: Macmillan pp. 31–53.

Humphries, Jane (1981) Protective Legislation, the Capitalist State and Working Class Men: the Case of the 1842 Mines Act. *Feminist Review* 7: 1–33.

Kirkham, Margaret (1983) *Jane Austen, Feminism and Fiction*. Brighton: The Harvester Press.

Liddell, Robert (1969) *The Novels of Jane Austen*. London: Longman.

Lovell, Terry (1978) Jane Austen and the Gentry. In Diana Laurenson (ed.) *The Sociology of Literature: Applied Studies*. Keele, Sociological Review Monographs 26: 15–37.

McRobbie, Angela (1978) Working Class Girls and the Culture of Femininity. In Women's Studies Group, Centre for Contemporary Cultural Studies (eds) *Women Take Issue*. London: Hutchinson pp. 96–108.

Mansell, Darrell (1973) *The Novels of Jane Austen: An Interpretation*. London: Macmillan.

Moers, Ellen (1974) Money, the Job, and Little Women. In Rose L. Coser (ed.) *The Family: its Structures and Functions*. London: Macmillan pp. 200–15.

Monaghan, David (ed.) (1981) *Jane Austen in a Social Context*. London: Macmillan.

Murray, Janet Horowitz (ed.) (1984) *Strong-Minded Women*. Harmondsworth: Penguin.

Poovey, Mary (1984) *The Proper Lady and the Woman Writer*. Chicago: University of Chicago Press.

Richardson *Clarissa*.

Rubinstein, E. (ed.) (1969) *Twentieth Century Interpretations of Pride and Prejudice*. Englewood Cliffs, N.J: Prentice Hall.

Schapera, I. (1977) *Kinship Terminology in Jane Austen's Novels*. London: Royal Anthropological Institute.

Stone, Laurence and Stone, J.C. Fawtier (1984) *An Open Elite? England 1540–1880.* Oxford: Oxford University Press.

Thompson, E.P. (1963) *The Making of the English Working Class.* London: Gollancz.

—— (1974) Patrician Society, Plebian Culture. *Journal of Social History* 7, 4: 383–405.

—— (1978) Eighteenth-century English Society: Class Struggle without Class? *Social History* 3, 2: 133–65.

Tolstoy, Leo *Anna Karenina.*

Name index

Subject index

Subject index

Subject index

liberalism 2, 65–6, 75

literature, and romance 47, 51–2

Lucas, Charlotte (*Pride and Prejudice*) 33–4

Mansfield Park 64, 87; metaphor for society 26, 70; Mrs Norris 1, 25, 61, 86; Mr Rushworth 25, 27, 31, 50, 52, 56, 71–4; *see also* Bertram family; Crawford family; Price family

marriage 1, 23–4, 56–8, 73, 78; economic security 7–8, 21, 45–6, 54; sexuality 14–16, 75

Marriages Act (1836) 74

Married Women's Property Act 21

men 64–80; and domestic life 58–62; masculine qualities 49–50; power 9–10, 44–5, 55; provision for women 9, 14–15, 18–19, 79–80; *see also* parents

middle class 13, 14

morality 2–3, 48–50, 82; bourgeois 11, 16–17, 57; and material world 20–1, 26–8, 35; sexual 12–16, 43–4, 52, 57, 72–5; *see also* education; equality; poverty; women

Morland, Catherine (*Northanger Abbey*) 39, 46–7

Musgrove family (*Persuasion*) 76

New Poor Law (1834) 74

Norris, Mrs (*Mansfield Park*) 1, 25, 61, 86

Northanger Abbey 39; Mrs Allen 39–40; Catherine Morland 39, 46–7; romance 47; Mr Tilney 47

parents: recognition of children 11, 14; repressive *see* Sir Thomas Bertram; responsibility 7, 60–3

patriarchal authority 2, 25, 49, 54–7, 61, 75

patriarchy 10–11, 30, 43–63

Persuasion 36, 64, 87; Admiral and Mrs Croft 36, 45, 68; Musgrove family 76; Lady Russell 68; Mrs Smith 8; Captain Wentworth 6–7, 9, 35, 38, 50, 59, 68, 86; *see also* Elliot family

pop songs 48

poverty 4–8, 28–9, 33, 83; moral 83–4

power 27–8, 66–7; men 9–10, 44–5, 55; sexual 29, 41, 55; women 9–10

Price, family (*Mansfield Park*) 6, 8, 59, 75, 85; Mr Price 60; Mrs Price 86; William 35, 68

Price Fanny 1, 6, 7, 49, 68, 71, 83; morality 25–30, 45, 52, 76–7; against patriarchy 30, 54–5

Pride and Prejudice: Mr Bingley 18; Mr Collins 33–4; Lady Catherine de Bourgh 32; Mr and Mrs Gardiner 38, 45; Charlotte Lucas 33–4; Mr Wickham 33, 47, 48, 61, 87; *see also* Bennet family; Mr Darcy

prison system 82–3

professions 18, 20

profit, accumulation of 3, 65, 66, 69, 77–80

property 18–42; control by men 11, 14, 58; maintenance 19–27, 34–6, 67; and morality 9–10, 27–8; and virtue 21–2, 33; and women 21–7

Subject index